Siblings in Late Permanent Placements

Siblings in Late Permanent Placements

Alan Rushton
Cherilyn Dance
David Quinton
Deborah Mayes

B *r i t i s h*
A *g e n c i e s*
for **A** *d o p t i o n*
and **F** *o s t e r i n g*

Published by
British Agencies for Adoption & Fostering
(BAAF)
Skyline House
200 Union Street
London SE1 0LX
www.baaf.org.uk

Charity registration 275689

**British Library Cataloguing in Publication
Data**
A catalogue record for this book is available
from the British Library

ISBN 1 873868 97 9

Editorial project management by Shaila Shah,
Head of Communications, BAAF
Photographs on cover by John Birdsall
    Photography www.JohnBirdsall.co.uk
Designed by Andrew Haig & Associates
Typeset by Avon Dataset Ltd, Bidford on Avon
Printed by Russell Press Ltd. (TU),
Nottingham

Notes about the authors

Alan Rushton, Senior Lecturer in Social Work, Institute of Psychiatry
was for many years a mental health social worker with children and adults in the UK and in Canada, and currently directs the MSc programme in Mental Health Social Work. He has conducted research into a range of social work topics including adoption and fostering, child protection and post-qualifying training. He is the author with colleagues of *New Parents for Older Children*, London: BAAF.

Cherilyn Dance, Research Co-ordinator, Maudsley Family Research Studies, Institute of Psychiatry, London
has a background in child health and has a degree in developmental psychology. She has been involved in a variety of placement related research studies since she joined the team in 1989. Her particular research interests concern the experiences of birth children in new families when older children are placed with them and placed children's experiences in the school system.

David Quinton, Professor of Psychosocial Development in the School for Policy Studies at the University of Bristol
has a background in anthropology and developmental psychopathology and has worked for many years on long-term outcome studies of people whose early experiences put them at risk for psychosocial problems. He is Director of the Hadley Centre for Adoption and Foster Care Studies at Bristol.

Deborah Mayes, Research Worker, Maudsley Family Research Studies, Institute of Psychiatry, London
Deborah was involved with this research between 1993 and 1997. Prior to joining the research team she worked as a child and family social worker in a London borough and as a researcher for the Economist Intelligence Unit.

The same research team co-authored *Joining New Families: A study of adoption and fostering in middle childhood*, Chichester: Wiley

Acknowledgements

First and most importantly, we should like to thank the families for seeing us at a time when their prime concern was getting to know the children. Without them this book would not have been possible. We are grateful to the agency managers who agreed to take part in the study and the social workers, both for helping us to make contact with the parents and for giving their time to talk about the placements. We were also greatly assisted by those schools that helped us recruit our comparison group. Finally, we wish to express our thanks to the Department of Health for funding the study and Dr Carolyn Davies, our research liaison officer, and her colleagues for their continued support and encouragement. Thanks are due also to Professor Roy Parker and his colleagues who commented on early drafts of this text, Sarah Borthwick of BAAF's Publications Advisory Group and anonymous readers who reviewed the text on behalf of the Department of Health and were most constructive in their comments.

Note

Use and management of illustrative material
In the course of writing the book, we have drawn on information provided in the course of the interviews to illustrate various points. Much of the time we have provided names for the children along with some general descriptive information in order that the example has a context. However, we would emphasise that we are most respectful of the privacy of those who took part in the study. Therefore, the names and details we provide have been changed in ways that serve to preserve anonymity without compromising the relevance of the material.

Contents

1 Sibling research and sibling placements

Introduction

As most children in the population have at least one sibling, it is not surprising to find that this is also true for children "looked after" in public care. Findings from various studies suggest that between 82 per cent and 87 per cent of looked after children in the UK have at least one sibling (Wedge and Phelan, 1986; Kosonen, 1996; Bilson and Barker, 1992/3). Concern as to the benefits and problems of placement with or without siblings should therefore be of major interest to child care professionals. Surprisingly, however, the topic has received little research attention. In this study, therefore, we wanted to bring sibling issues to centre stage in family placement research. Our special concern was with children who had been placed late in permanent, unrelated family homes and to contrast those placed singly with those placed with some or all of their siblings.

We begin by briefly reviewing current policy and practice guidance on the placement of siblings. This is followed by a consideration of some of the methodological difficulties inherent in investigating sibling placements. We then go on to discuss what is known about outcomes for children placed on their own or with their siblings. Finally, we consider how relationships between siblings may be affected by the children's earlier experiences and how the quality of their relationships may have an impact on the security of placement. This discussion necessarily relies on what is known about sibling relationships in birth-parent families because of the lack of research on adopted and fostered siblings. The focus of this review is mainly on middle childhood, since the majority of the children in this study fall into this age range.

Policy, law and sibling placements

The main policy guidance on the placement of sibling groups is found in the Children Act 1989. This states that siblings should be accommodated together whenever 'reasonably practicable and consistent with the child's welfare' (section 23 (7)(b)). Why has this preference now been written into legislation? Two distinct arguments have been advanced. Research in developmental psychology has shown that the presence of birth siblings can be mutually supportive and that the separation from or loss of these important relationships can have negative effects (Dunn and McGuire, 1992). Keeping sibling groups together has also been argued on the basis of *rights* (O'Leary and Schofield, 1994). Both of these arguments provide strong reasons for keeping siblings together. However, the placement of children in alternative families raises distinct issues because of the atypicality of their earlier experiences. In the absence of good research evidence it is important to note some of the arguments against keeping siblings together. For example, such placements may not be 'consistent with the children's welfare' when one sibling has physically or sexually abused another and may do so again. Again, a child may express a strong wish to be placed separately from one or more siblings and this has to be taken into account. Finally, if intense friction between siblings jeopardises placement stability or the children's psychosocial development, placement together may be inadvisable.

One of the commonest arguments for splitting sibling groups is that the level of emotional or behavioural disturbance in one or more children is such that their combined needs are unlikely to be met when parental attention has to be divided between them. One consequence of this may be that the placements are more prone to disruption. A further common consideration is that delays in finding a family able to care for a large sibling group may keep the children in indeterminate placements and thus not be in their interests. In child welfare practice it is often not simply a matter of following one clear option but of deciding which of several principles are to be given most weight. For example, taking the option to re-unite a sibling group may secure the benefits of living together, but may also involve the breaking of established attachments.

Such judgements on the benefits and drawbacks of different placements are made by child care workers, consultants and placement panels on a daily basis but as yet there is little research on the quality of sibling relationships and the outcome of sibling placements to guide them. Practitioner assumptions about placement choices need to be identified and tested. Better guidance is needed on when or whether to split, maintain or reunite a group of siblings. More detailed information is needed on the progress of children who are placed together or on their own. More needs to be known about the effects on birth and placed children when a placement leads to new sibling relationships.

In order to answer these questions, adequate and wide-ranging descriptive data on sibling relationships are required as well as a better understanding of how to categorise and analyse such data.

Definitions and measurement of sibling relationships

Before turning to the relevant research on sibling relationships, it is necessary to examine some key issues of terminology and methodology. The most fundamental of these, although the answer may seem obvious, is the definition of a sibling. Siblings are, by definition, usually biologically related, with full siblings being the product of the same set of parents and half-siblings sharing one parent. But increasingly many genetically unrelated children are growing up together as step-siblings. For some, there may be a legal relationship with the unrelated parent by virtue of adoption. Clearly there are potential differences in the way these relationships are perceived by the children, their parents and the wider society and these need to be borne in mind when planning research and interpreting research findings.

Even among the general population, sibling constellations can rapidly become quite elaborate, with new partnerships and further births leading to a sibling group with a mixture of relationships. However, as Staff, Fein and Johnson (1993) have pointed out, these issues become even more complex for children who are, or have been, looked after by local authorities. Children from the same family are often separated, at least for periods, while in care. They may, in addition, be placed for several years with families who have other children at home. Children may also be growing up in their birth families; some of the children may have been born after the placed children entered care and may not be known by the latter. For these reasons, the question of whether a sibling relationship should be defined by biology or experience becomes paramount for both practice and research. From a research perspective, trying to take account of all possible permutations of children's "sibling" experiences is beset with problems and may account for much of the slow progress in examining sibling placements. However, reliable information is greatly needed and there must be agreed definitions of sibling constellations in order for research to proceed.

Sibling issues in permanent placement

Only recently has the issue of siblings in substitute care become a focus for research and there are a number of questions that are yet to be fully addressed. There has been no recent, comprehensive, critical review of empirical studies on the progress of sibling placements, in part perhaps because there has not been a great deal to review. There is good evidence on the frequency of sibling placements and a steadily growing practice literature but little beyond this.

Frequency of sibling placements

As already outlined, the majority of older children who require permanent placement can be expected to have brothers and sisters and many of these brothers and sisters will also need permanent substitute care. The recent report from BAAF (Ivaldi, 2000), which surveyed the adoption records of over three-quarters of the local authorities in England and Wales, found that 37 per cent of all children adopted during 1998/9 were placed as part of a sibling group. These data also suggest that around one-fifth of adoptive families had sibling groups placed with them. This proportion is somewhat higher than the proportion of children jointly referred in Wedge and Mantle's earlier study (1991).

Studies of the permanent placement of children who are older or who have special needs have also found a high proportion placed as sibling groups. This was so for one-third of the children in our own recent study

(Quinton *et al*, 1998) and for 40 per cent of children in the study by Fratter and her colleagues (1991) of 1,165 permanent family placements of children in the UK with "special needs".

Practitioner research

Practitioner research, although on the increase, is commonly based on single case examples accompanied by a discussion of the issues raised. Many of these papers lament the lack of attention to sibling issues in the placement literature. The practice papers have so far addressed questions like: practitioners' motivations for keeping siblings together (Morrison and Brown, 1986); the importance of maintaining bonds between siblings (Ward, 1984; Mapp, 1995); assessing siblings for family placement (Bellwood, 1985); considerations arising when placing a single child from a sibling group in care (Timberlake and Hamlin, 1982); the implications of changing the birth order of siblings (Nix, 1983); and the relationship between theoretical knowledge and decision making (Jones and Niblett, 1985). Occasional papers have addressed therapeutic interventions involving sibling groups (Lewis, 1986; Rosenberg, 1988; Hindle, 1995). However, these questions have yet to be taken forward in systematic research, despite the fact that practitioners have been raising them for several years.

Placement outcomes for sibling groups and singly placed children

Although there have been few studies specifically dedicated to sibling placements, several studies with a wider focus have commented on outcomes according to whether children are placed with siblings or not. The majority of these studies have reported a tendency for sibling placements to have better outcomes, either in being less likely to disrupt or in showing higher levels of new parent satisfaction or lower levels of child problems (Barth and Berry, 1988; Berridge and Cleaver, 1987; Festinger, 1986; Groze, 1996; Holloway, 1997; Kagan and Reid, 1986; Quinton *et al*, 1998). However, the findings are often complex and show both advantages and problems in placement choice. Notable exceptions also exist. Parker (1966) found few differences in the outcomes for sibling placements and separated children while among Kadushin and Siedl's (1971) sample, separated children did better.

In 1987, Berridge and Cleaver reported that their investigation of long-term foster family care in the UK revealed higher rates of break-down for those placed away from siblings. The placements of half of the 64 children with siblings in care but not living with them broke down: a much higher rate than for those accompanied by brothers and sisters. They concluded that the presence of familiar others may have helped to relieve some of the stresses on the children (p. 81). However, this is only one of many possible causal explanations for this finding. The study was not in a position to control for the children's behavioural difficulties, past histories and experiences or for other factors associated with single placements.

Studies that have focused more specifically on sibling aspects of placement have also produced mixed findings. Staff and Fein (1992) studied 262 children aged 5–13 years in a private fostering agency in the USA. Disruption rates were similar for children placed with their siblings and those children who had no siblings (only children), but those who were separated from brothers or sisters tended to do less well. One possible confounder was that younger children were more likely to be placed with their siblings and this might explain the differences. Even if it does not, the authors warn that the work in this agency was particularly well resourced with small case loads. For this reason the findings may not generalise to other settings. In addition, they were only able to judge outcomes through disruption rates.

Wedge and Mantle (1991) studied sibling groups who were referred for permanent placement. A minority of their sample was separated from siblings and placed separately. They reported a 21 per cent disruption rate both for the children placed with their siblings and those separated from them. Younger siblings had a higher disruption rate than had been found by others (Thoburn and Rowe, 1988). They suggested that some-times the younger children's placements might have been more in jeopardy because of the problems of their older siblings, while in other cases being placed with a younger sibling may reduce the chance of an older sibling being rejected by the new family.

Thorpe and Swart (1992) conducted a retrospective pilot study using record searches to study 115 siblings from 48 families from infancy to 15 years old in Canada. The children were mainly suffering from neglect rather than abuse. They excluded children who came into care at different points in time, or who were placed apart, those who were not full siblings and those for whom separation had been due to behavioural problems. They wished to determine whether or not siblings placed together protected one another. They found that separated siblings fared better, when they used "number of symptoms" and "school functioning" as the outcome measure. A drawback to this study was its retrospective nature and a lack of any severity ratings on childhood problems. The authors speculated that the singly placed children thrived on individual attention and found it easier to ally with adult caregivers.

Groze (1996) reported complex findings where the socio-emotional outcomes for singly placed children were poorer than for children placed with siblings but the relationships between the parents and children were better. He suggested that this may have reflected the difficulty for parents in forming a new relationship with more than one child at a time. Unfortunately, the response rate in this longitudinal study had begun well but only 25 per cent of the original sample were represented by the end of the fourth year. For this reason the findings on outcomes and factors related to them must be treated with caution.

The studies mentioned above cover a long period of child welfare practice and some of the differences might have been due to changes in placement policy and practice. However, it is also possible that there is an effect of age at placement. Many of the studies that have found outcomes to be poorer for singly placed or separated children have sampled older children, while the majority of the other studies have included the entire age range.

One area where there is much more consensus is that placements appear to be particularly vulnerable when children are placed with families that already have birth children in the home (Barth and Berry, 1988). This has been found especially true if the placement violates the "golden rule": that is, when the child placed is either older than, or less than three or four years younger than, the youngest of the existing children (Trasler, 1960; Parker, 1966; Wedge and Mantle, 1991). However, Berridge and Cleaver (1987) noted placements of this kind were frequently made even though social workers were familiar with this risk.

Interestingly, the findings about existing birth children may not be as strong for sibling groups as for children placed on their own (Boer and Spiering, 1991; Quinton *et al*, 1998).

The findings reported by many studies about the relative success of sibling group placements, may have influenced policy makers to emphasise the maintenance of sibling groups in placement wherever practical. However, as pointed out earlier, there are occasions when arguments for separation of children may outweigh those in favour of maintenance of a sibling group. This being the case, a number of questions remain to be addressed. What is it about being singly placed that may increase the risk of poorer placement outcome? What is happening in placements where singly placed children join established families? How important is the character of the relationship between siblings?

Differences between sibling groups and singly placed children
In the light of the findings outlined above, the first question to tackle is whether singly placed children differ in important ways from those who are with their siblings. If they do, then the findings on better outcomes for sibling placements may simply be a reflection of differences between singly placed children and sibling groups. The suggestion that *only* children are not at greater risk points in this direction.

It is necessary, to begin with, to define terms. Children may be placed on their own because they simply do not have any siblings, because they have no siblings who are being looked after, or because a decision has been made to separate them from siblings who are looked after elsewhere. It is likely that these three reasons for being placed alone generate very different feelings for the children and for those planning or caring for them. Where researchers have observed these distinctions, it appears that children who have no siblings do relatively well in placement (Staff and Fein, 1992), while children who are separated from siblings have more difficulties.

The work of Aldridge and Cautley (1976) gave an early indication that comparisons between outcomes for separated and jointly-placed children may be complicated by a variety of factors. They studied the placements of 115 children aged between 6 and 12 years old. Fifty-five of these index children were placed with at least one sibling and the remainder were placed alone. Data were collected from foster carers and social workers at fixed points over the first 18 months of placement. They found that a similar proportion of joint and singleton placements was described as progressing very well at the final interview, but that a larger proportion of placements of children placed without siblings were assessed as working out poorly. They concluded that placing siblings together did not undermine the placement but observed that the better than average pre-placement experiences of these children might also explain the positive effect. Siblings who were placed together were more likely to be girls; had fewer moves; were less disturbed and were less likely to have been rejected by a birth parent. The outcome measures were limited to foster carer and social work reports on whether the siblings were having a positive or negative effect on one another, whether the placement was intact, and how it was viewed by the worker and carer involved.

Only two studies have measures of children's behaviour at the beginning of placement. A pilot study of 18 boys placed in middle childhood (Rushton, Treseder, and Quinton, 1989) found that children placed with siblings made better progress than those placed alone, but the latter differed in having higher initial problem levels. All of the singly placed boys were separated from at least one sibling who was placed elsewhere.

These findings were replicated in our more recent study, which followed the first year of placement of 61 children who were placed for permanence between the ages of 5 and 9 (Quinton, Rushton, Dance and Mayes, 1998). Thirty-four percent of these children were placed with at least one brother or sister. Two outcome measures were used: the children's level of developmental recovery and a variable combining the new parents' level of satisfaction with the quality of the parent–child relationship. Poorer outcomes on both these measures were evident for singly placed children. This was particularly true when the children's siblings remained in the birth home and the placed child had experienced rejection by birth parents.

Boer, Westenberg and Ooyen-Houben (1995) examined the first admission to care for a group of children who were admitted with siblings and a second group who were admitted alone. Children placed in both residential and foster care were included. These authors found marked differences between the groups in the characteristics of the children and their family backgrounds. Children who were entering care alone were much more likely to be male; to come from a two-parent family; and to have behavioural problems and difficulties in the parent–child relationship. The reason for entry to care was more likely to be child related, at least in part, than was true for jointly placed children. This study was able to offer information about one group of separated children only: those whose siblings were *all* with the family of origin at the time of entry to care. However, the findings highlight the fact that the success of placements of separated and jointly placed children cannot be compared without reference to their earlier experiences.

Children joining established families
There are a number of reasons why placement with an established family might be more complex than joining a child-free family. In the first place an increased number of new relationships will have to be negotiated by the child. In addition, the relationships between existing family members are also likely to change as a result of the arrival of a new child (Pinderhughes, 1996). Some of these relationships will be with children already in the family and they may approach the placement with a different perspective from their parents or a more limited ability to adapt to the new relationships.

A study of infant adoptions by families with and without birth children was undertaken by Hoopes (1982) who found that mixed families' children (that is families with both birth and placed children) were more defiant, hostile and reckless. The parents were less encouraging towards the child and the whole family faced more complex tasks of integration and identity formation. It was reported that these families had the greatest difficulty in parental functioning.

Wedge and Mantle's (1991) study of jointly placed and separated siblings found that siblings fared better in child-free homes and suggested that this arrangement might have led to better sibling relations and less stress on parents. In their sample, 35 per cent of the placements contained between one and four resident children. Of the 28 placements that disrupted, the foster carers' conflict of loyalty between meeting the needs of their own children and the placed children was given as the fourth

SIBLING RESEARCH AND SIBLING PLACEMENTS

most commonly mentioned contributory factor. However, where children were placed in existing families, their research reinforced Parker's finding (1966) that a large age gap between placed and new siblings had a protective effect.

In our own recent study (Quinton *et al*, 1998) poorer outcomes for singly placed children were particularly prominent where they joined an established family and among these placements difficulties between the placed children and the families' birth children were relatively frequent. In part, this study confirmed the findings of others (Parker, 1966; Wedge and Mantle, 1991) that, where the placed child was older or close in age to the youngest child, placements were more prone to poorer outcomes. However, in this study sibling relationship difficulties were not confined to placements with small age gaps. Significant problems also arose where the birth sibling was an adolescent. These adjustment problems for adolescent birth children were rarely associated with poorer placement stability but they could cause considerable strain for the families. Although there is considerable evidence that placing children with established families can be problematic, there has been little detailed attention paid to the way the resident children respond and the subsequent patterns of interaction between the children.

Placement decisions and contact between separated siblings

Where only one child enters care there is clearly no option about placing them on their own but it is clear that many placed children have siblings looked after elsewhere in the care system. Kosonen (1996) reported the findings of a study of one Scottish local authority where, of 260 children who had siblings they were not placed with, 125 had siblings looked after elsewhere. Bilson and Barker (1992/3) found that, of 539 children who had siblings who were also in care, only 25 per cent were placed with all their brothers and sisters and 42 per cent were not placed with any siblings.

The factors most frequently mentioned by social workers as important in decisions to maintain sibling groups, are the mutual bond between the children, the degree of difficulty they present, and the influence of the birth parents (Boer and Spiering, 1991). Reasons for separation tend to focus on the needs of individual children, although children's views and limited placement availability may also play a part (Wedge and Mantle, 1991). In Kosonen's study (1996), the most frequent reason for separation was that the siblings had entered care at different times. From her analysis Kosonen concluded that points of entering and leaving care, whether for return home, independence or for adoption, were especially likely to be associated with separation of siblings. Bilson and Barker found that three-quarters of the children placed with some or all of their siblings were in their first or second placement while a quarter of the children placed away from siblings had five or more placements.

Accepting that separation is sometimes unavoidable, the next issue that arises is sibling contact. Bilson and Barker (1992/93) found that when siblings remain with the birth family, contact is likely to be dictated by levels of contact with birth parents. As with the pattern found by Millham *et al* (1986) for birth parents, the frequency of contact decreased the longer a child was in care: 70 per cent of children looked after for less than a year having had contact at least monthly with their siblings at home, although this proportion dropped to 35 per cent after five or more years in care. Contact with siblings who were elsewhere in the care system was even less frequent. Only 25 per cent of children who had been looked after for five or more years were in at least monthly contact.

The studies by Kosonen and Bilson and Barker both present data on all looked after children, and therefore include those who are in short-term, long-term or permanent placement. It is likely that children who are placed for permanence have even lower levels of sibling contact than those in these studies.

Sibling relationships for children in placement

The family patterns of children in care can be especially complex. The children may have full, half- and step-siblings, any of whom may be with birth parent/s, extended family or elsewhere within the care system. They may even have siblings they have not met or do not even know about. Taking these variations into account is a considerable research challenge, but, in addition, older children who are about to embark on a permanent placement will probably have spent at least some time in other foster families and may have lived with other children whom they have come to regard as brothers or sisters. Although it is unlikely that any study could include such additional complexity, it is a feature of children's experience which should be considered by practitioners in individual cases.

The potential diversity of biological, legal and psychological relationships means that it is essential to begin to focus on what is important about sibling relationships for looked after children. This has hardly begun in research beyond the small-scale practitioner accounts discussed earlier. Wedge and Mantle (1991) noted the lack of information in social work records concerning patterns of sibling interaction. They could find no obvious link between social work judgements about the quality of sibling relationships and the decision to split sibling groups. They found that the usual aim was to try to maintain groups whatever the relationship.

Studies that have explored the views, memories and feelings of adults who have grown up in the care system have found that separation from siblings was frequently a painful experience whereas those who stayed with siblings saw this as a source of comfort. Maintenance of sibling groups in the care system, wherever possible, is seen as desirable from a number of viewpoints. It provides an element of continuity and an anchor point with the family of origin; siblings placed together may be able to share memories and experiences and offer each other support. However, the whole sibling placement may be difficult to sustain if there are negative interactions between siblings.

Kosonen (1994) cites children's individual needs and disruption of a joint placement as the primary reason for separation. Although not expressly stated, it is likely that the relationship between the siblings in these cases was found to be insufficient to warrant perseverance with a plan of joint placement. We have found no studies to date which have examined the relationship between placed children to determine whether relationships differ between looked after siblings and those growing up with their own families, and the extent to which any differences may have an impact on placement stability.

Although these aspects have not so far been explored among looked

13

after populations, there is sufficient evidence from research with other samples to suggest that the sibling relationships of children who require permanent placement may differ in important ways from those of children growing up in their own homes. It is crucial to learn more about the way siblings get along together and the ways in which their experiences may have altered the usual balance of their relationship.

Research into sibling relationships in non-placed samples

Empirical research into sibling relationships in the general population began to expand in the 1960s. Studies have highlighted how interaction between siblings can have a powerful impact on the experience of managing conflict, on the development of pro-social behaviours, and on the development of social understanding: that is, developing an appreciation of the perspectives and feelings of others (Dunn and McGuire, 1992).

In terms of measuring the characteristics of sibling relationships, the ideal would be to collect information from multiple sources including the children themselves (Graham-Bermann, 1994). However, this is not always possible and although interactions between children can be observed by others, Graham-Bermann's (1994) results suggest that it is likely that conflict may be underestimated and co-operation over-estimated by outsiders.

In order to examine the influence of sibling relationships it is necessary first to identify some key features. Furman and Buhrmester (1985) undertook this task through interviews with children about their relationships with a sibling. They found four features that were central to describing sibling relationships. These were: the degree of warmth, conflict and rivalry, and the "relative power" in the relationship, that is, the extent to which one of the siblings nurtured or dominated the other. Stormshak and colleagues (1996) suggest descriptive categories of sibling relationship according to the balance between warmth and conflict – high conflict/low warmth; balanced conflict and warmth; low conflict/high warmth.

Rivalry and conflict are both normal elements of a sibling relationship, indeed it is suggested that aggression between siblings might lead to the development of successful control of aggressive motivation since the sibling relationship does not break under the strain as peer relationships might (Bryant, 1982; Raffaelli, 1991).

While sibling relationships are widely assumed to be important in the long term, since they are likely to be the longest lasting relationship most people experience, findings are inconsistent concerning the developmental course of sibling relationships. It is known that sibling relationships, like those with parents, often become less important than peer relationships during adolescence (Burhmester and Furman, 1990) but there is a growing body of evidence that, for most people, the importance of sibling relationships lasts through adulthood and into old age (Cicirelli, 1994).

Parentification or sibling to sibling caregiving

In most families older siblings take some responsibility for their younger brothers and sisters, offer some elements of care and control, and at times provide for the needs of the younger ones. Kosonen (1996) found that 70 per cent of 9–12-year-old children admitted to receiving care from an older sibling and 55 per cent had cared for a younger sibling. For the most part, the children liked being cared for *by* and caring *for* their siblings, although the author warns that there is a serious possibility of danger of sibling to sibling abuse. Cicirelli (1973) found that younger siblings were more likely to accept help from an older sister than an older brother and were more likely to accept help from a sibling who was four years older than one who was only two years older. Bryant and Crockenberg (1980) found that the caretaking sibling was usually the oldest child and tended to adopt the directive style of their mother, but lacked the skills to carry this off in a positive way. They were more likely to give negative help and encouragement, and their help was not always appreciated by the younger siblings. Older caretaking siblings used punishment more than their parents. This was thought to arise from their lack of helping strategies. Younger siblings may well fight against an older sibling who tried to foster dependency, especially if this was seen as controlling or bossy, rather than facilitating.

However, the effect on the younger children can also have a positive side. Bryant (1992) found that children who received sibling caretaking had better peer interactions because they were more accepting of individual differences in their peers. To date there does not appear to have been any research on the developmental consequences for the caretaking child, although Miller and Cantwell's (1986) research suggests that siblings can positively influence the development of a troubled sibling.

The extent to which caretaking happens in families will probably vary according to the availability of the parent, the ages of the children involved, and the culture in which the children are growing up. Bank and Kahn (1982a, b) have written extensively about the ways in which caregiving may develop in families where the children feel abandoned by parents or where strains between parents are evident. Caregiving may be a child's attempt to contain stresses or to retain the family's identity. In their work with adult siblings, these authors found that one-way caregiving roles could become extremely rigid and have negative consequences for both the carer and the cared for. Clearly these factors may apply to looked after children. The risk of maladaptive caring roles for groups of siblings in care must be significant.

Factors influencing the quality of sibling relationships

A number of relevant issues have been explored by researchers interested in the relationships between brothers and sisters. The evidence suggests that the quality of relationship between the children and the parent/s is an important determinant of sibling relationships as are the temperamental characteristics of the children, particularly the oldest in a dyad, with more conflictual relationships noted for children with "difficult" temperaments. Kosonen (1994) has suggested that children who are close in age or of the same gender – that is, those with "high access" to each other – may develop an emotionally intense relationship which may be more prone to conflict. Sibling relationship difficulties have also been found to be associated with marital discord (Brody et al, 1987) and with parental separation (Zill, 1988).

A related but different line of enquiry has been to explore the effect of parental intervention in the interaction between siblings. Rivalry, conflict and warmth between siblings have all been found to vary according to the way in which parents handle their children. Although there is some inconsistency in the findings concerning warmth, higher levels of maternal differential treatment has been linked to high levels of conflict between siblings (Boer and Dunn, 1992; Dunn, Stocker and Plomin, 1989). The link may be especially strong where families are under stress. The differential treatment of siblings by their mother has been found to lead to ill will between the siblings generated both by the child who is shunned and the child who is favoured (Bryant and Crockenberg, 1980).

Maternal intervention in conflict has been found to be associated with higher levels of conflict between siblings, although this finding has been widely assumed to indicate that maternal intervention leads to the increase, firstly by providing maternal attention and secondly by depriving children of the opportunity to resolve their conflicts. The direction of the link is yet to be established, since it is possible that parents respond to intensity of conflict and that siblings who have serious disputes also have them frequently (Dunn and McGuire, 1992). Although there is more consistency in findings about the negative aspects of sibling relationships, Boer and Dunn (1992) reported an association between positive parental care and positive sibling relationships.

Sibling relationships and negative life experiences
Of greater relevance to our area of interest is the limited number of studies that have examined sibling relationships in adversity. This topic is addressed because the current study is concerned with children from high risk backgrounds who will have endured separations and losses. Do these experiences make sibling relationships weaker or stronger, closer or more distant, supportive or rivalrous?

Freud and Dann's (1951) work with orphaned children during the war is often quoted as they believed that external stress strengthened the sibling bond and they observed the children becoming more concerned and protective towards each other. In a small retrospective study, Bank and Kahn (1982a) studied videotaped interviews of siblings who grew up under conditions of parental loss and emotional hardship and concluded that parental unavailability appeared to promote intense loyalty and devotion. However, Bank (1992) suggests that this intense bonding is not always positive and the tie which may develop as a result of traumatic experiences may be warm but also clinging, fearful, ambivalent, violently negative or marked by disappointment.

It is quite feasible that pre-existing good relationships between children may protect them and encourage further closeness in times of stress, but this must be set against the background of the work reviewed earlier which suggests that poor parenting practices, family disharmony or difficult parent–child relationships may inhibit the development of good relationships in the first place. If the family atmosphere is tense and argumentative, there may be negative effects on individual children and consequently on their relationships. Indeed, they may model their behaviour on the warring adults.

Kier and Lewis (1998) have labelled these two viewpoints the 'protection against adversity hypothesis' and the 'family pathology' hypothesis. They argue that the effect on siblings will depend on the nature of the stress and the age and sex constellation. For example, much may depend on whether there is an older sister who takes on a nurturing role toward the younger siblings.

The relevance to placed samples
Previous research suggests that children who are in need of permanent family placement will be more likely than most children to have witnessed or experienced marital disputes, economic hardship, parental ill health, and poor parenting. They will certainly have experienced separation from their families and, in all probability, from at least some of their siblings. The ways in which these experiences may have an impact on the development of relationships between the children has been discussed by Kosonen (1994). It is likely that through these experiences, certain patterns of sibling interaction are acquired and reinforced according to family circumstances, constellations and emotional atmosphere, and that these contribute to a "sibling culture" which accompanies the children when they move to a new placement. This will influence how they accommodate to new parents and possibly to new siblings.

Sibling issues for new parents

In the same way as there are sibling considerations for most children who have been looked after, regardless of the new family constellation, there will be issues concerning siblings for most new parents. Either they will be caring for a jointly placed sibling group, or trying to help a singly placed child integrate with their own children, or helping children to manage the fact of their separation from siblings and maintain an element of contact with them wherever possible. For placements where there are two or more children in the family home, it is likely that the relationships between the children will have important consequences for the way the family functions.

From the preceding review it is clear that children, whether placed separately or together, may enter placement with patterns of interaction that lead to difficulties for parents. In preparing prospective parents and supporting placements, much more needs to be learned about the relationships between children, how these may change and develop in placement, and whether there are features of the relationship that may jeopardise placements.

Overview

Research into sibling placements has received less attention than other aspects of permanent placement research and previous studies have only been partially successful in dealing with the considerable methodological and data collection problems involved. In terms of social work decision making, questions remain concerning the separation or maintenance of sibling groups and the placement options available for both sibling groups and separated children. From the perspective of preparation and support of substitute families, it is essential that knowledge is increased concerning the extent to which relationships between placed children differ from those of other groups of siblings and the effect that those relationships may have on the stability of the placement.

The examination of substitute family placements can potentially be directed at numerous questions, but any one research design can bear only so much weight. The greater the number of questions that we attempt to answer, the greater the risk that each is only partially answered.

In this study it was necessary, from the start, to favour some questions at the expense of others. In this report the main focus is on documenting sibling relationships and their effects. The contribution of factors like parenting style and the social work service receive less attention.

KEY POINTS
Sibling research and sibling placements

- Over 80 per cent of looked after children may be expected to have siblings, though not all will be in local authority care.

- Few studies have specifically aimed to explore differences in outcome according to whether children are placed with or without siblings, but several have commented on this. Evidence is not unanimous but leans towards better outcomes for those placed with siblings. However, this may be due not to differences in the placement constellation per se but to differences in the characteristics and histories of the two groups.

- Decisions about separation or maintenance are made at present without strong evidence-based guidance.

- Better understanding is needed of sibling interactions and relationships in new family placements to make sense of differing outcomes.

- It is likely that contact between separated siblings placed for permanence is low but this is under-researched.

---

2   Aims, design and methods

In the preceding chapter we outlined how little was known about siblings in permanent placement, despite the fact that a number of studies have found differences in outcome for children who are separated from siblings and those who are placed with them. In designing this study, we wished to examine a sample of permanent placements and to focus on sibling interactions and relationships. We were very conscious that while some children will be separated from their siblings during the process of placement, many others will gain new brothers and sisters. For this reason the study was designed to allow many permutations of separation, reunion, maintenance and creation of sibling groups to be assessed. The specific aims of the research were as follows:

- To investigate the whereabouts, circumstances and contact arrangements of birth siblings who are not with the placed children.
- To study how social work decisions on the separation, reunion or maintenance of siblings come about.
- To examine placement outcomes for children placed with or without siblings.
- To explore the relationships between brothers and sisters placed together and between those who became "new siblings" to each other as a result of placement with established families (that is, those who had birth children at home prior to placement).
- To compare the sibling relationships of placed children with children growing up in their birth families.
- To examine the impact of placement on the birth children of the new families.
- To document the level of post-placement social work intervention with particular reference to sibling issues.

Design

The study was prospective in design, taking referrals from participating local authorities at the time a match was agreed and tracking the families' experiences over the first year of the placement. The aim was to collect a consecutive sample of placements from each of the authorities but, despite considerable liaison and negotiation to encourage referral of all suitable cases, we could not be certain that this aim was met.

The sample included adoptive and permanent foster placements. A "sibling group placement" was defined as a placement of two or more biologically related children. In order to maintain comparability with our earlier study (Quinton et al, 1998) and to avoid the problems that might arise through sampling too wide an age range, at least one child had to be between the ages of 5 and 11 years at the time of placement. We excluded children with severe physical or learning disability because they present a different kind of parenting challenge and taking consecutive samples would not yield sufficient children for analyses. We also excluded placements where the parents had adopted or foster children living in the home in order to reduce the complexity of sibling patterns.

Data were collected from social workers, new parents and school teachers at three and 12 months after placement. New parents participated in face-to-face, home-based interviews at both points in time. Social workers were seen at three months and interviewed by telephone at 12 months. Teachers completed a brief questionnaire on each occasion. Seventy-two families, caring for 133 placed children and 28 resident birth children, took part in the study.

Referral procedure and comparison of participating and non-participating cases

A total of 24 home-finding agencies agreed to take part in the study, although only 16 of these made referrals. The agencies were situated around London and the Home Counties and included both local authorities and local branches of some of the larger voluntary placement agencies.

The agencies were asked to tell the research team of children meeting the sampling criteria at the time that a "match" was found between them and a new family. The social worker's help was then sought in making contact with the new parents. No details were passed to the research team until the consent of the family had been obtained. Ensuring that all eligible cases were referred required substantial effort and involved regular and time-consuming liaison with nominated contacts in each authority. Referrals to the study were received over a 21-month period. The 16 referring agencies were made up of nine county councils, four London boroughs (three inner, one outer) and three voluntary adoption agencies. They varied in their referral rates. The average number of referrals was seven (range 1 to 14). A total of 97 suitable referrals were received, of which 95 proceeded to placement. Of these, 23 could not be included: six disrupted very soon after placement; seven families declined to take part, and in 10 cases social workers declined to approach the families, usually because they felt the placement was already under stress. Anonymised data were obtained from social workers for these non-participating cases and the data on disruptions contained in Table 2.1 gives some support to their fears.

Table 2.1 provides a comparison of participating, non-participating and early disrupted placements on a number of characteristics. The groups did not differ on the majority of these but two features deserve comment. Established families were less likely to become part of the study, although not significantly so, whereas placements involving one or more sexually abused children were significantly more likely to be included. It is unclear why the parents taking sexually abused children should be over-represented in the sample. It is possible that this is linked to the lower proportion of established families. Perhaps, social workers tried to place sexually abused children in child-free homes if they feared that the children might be a danger to new siblings.

The other obvious difference between participating and non-participating families was in the frequency of disruption. Six cases disrupted before a first interview was due (column 3). Seven of the 17 non-participating cases disrupted by the first anniversary of placement (column 2). Thus, in total, 13 of the 23 eligible placements that did not enter the study (56 per cent) disrupted within the first year compared with 10 per cent of participating cases (Fisher's exact test 0.0002). The disruption rate, if calculated on all eligible cases – participants, non-participants and early disruptions (95 cases) – is in the region of 21 per cent. This rate is based on the number of "placements", these being defined as the placement of one or more children with one family.

23

Table 2.1
Characteristics of participating and non-participating cases

Characteristic	Sample (72)	Non-participants (17)	Early disruptions (6)
Singleton placement	44%	50%	38%
Minority ethnic origin	11%	17%	0%
Physical abuse	46%	47%	33%
Sexual abuse	43%	18%	17%
Emotional abuse	83%	71%	50%
Neglect	80%	82%	100%
Other siblings elsewhere	67%	76%	17%
All other sibs with birth family	50% (of 67%)	38% (of 76%)	data unreliable
Lone parent household (new)	0%	9%	0%
Minority ethnicity or dual heritage family	8%	15%	0%
Foster placement	21%	17%	13%
Established family	29%	47%	25%
Problematic relationship with new sibling/s	33% (of those with new sibs)	25% (of those with new sibs)	100% (of those with new sibs)
Disrupted placement	10%	30%	100%

The sample

Seventy-two families took part in interviews at three months into the placement. All but one of the households that the children joined were headed by couples and almost all of these were married. The average age of the mothers in the sample was just over 40 (ranging from 29 to 59 years, s.d. = 6.5). Fathers were just under 43 years old, on average (32–64 years, s.d. = 7.2). Couples had been together between one and 34 years (mean 12.7 years, s.d. = 7.7). The majority of families comprised two white parents, just four were headed by dual heritage couples, (either one white and one Asian parent or one white and one African/ African-Caribbean parent). Just over half the families approached the placement with no parenting experience at all, in a small number of cases (6) one parent had experience from a previous relationship, and in nearly 40 per cent of cases both adults had parented before.

Between them these families had a total of 133 placed children and 28 resident birth children. Thirty-two of the 133 children were placed singly, 19 in child-free homes and 13 in established families. There were 40 sibling groups. Thirty-six of these moved into child-free families (90 children in groups of two, three or four). The remaining four sibling groups (11 children in groups of two, three or four) joined a family with one or two birth children (Fig. 2.1).

Figure 2.1
The children and their placements

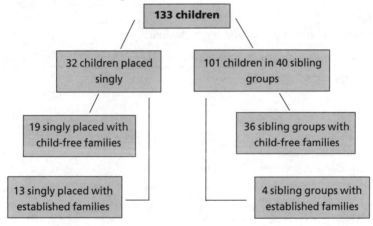

Table 2.2 compares the demographic characteristics of the placed and birth children. There were few differences apart from age, with three-quarters of the birth children being over 10 years of age compared with just 20 per cent of the placed children. This is in line with practice guidance that an incoming child should be substantially younger than resident birth children.

Apart from one Southern European child, all of the placed children with a minority ethnic background were of dual heritage, whereas the two minority ethnic birth children were born of "same race" couples. However, both of these birth children were living with a white step-parent at the time of the study.

Extent of transracial placement
There were five single children and three siblings groups where all of the children had a minority ethnic background. Of these, four of the five single children and one of the sibling groups were placed with a white family. In one further sibling group just one child had a minority heritage; these children were also placed with a white family. Overall, of 14 children with a minority background, eight were placed transracially. Interestingly there was one case in which two white children were placed with a dual heritage family.

Table 2.2
Characteristics of placed and birth children

Child characteristic	Placed children (n = 133) %	Birth children (n = 28) %
Gender		
Boys	50	54
Girls	50	46
Ethnic status		
2 white UK parents	89	93
2 African or A/C parents	0	7
2 S. European parents	1	0
1 white +1 Asian parent	4	0
1 white + 1 A/C parent	4	0
1 white + 1 African parent	2	0
Age		
Under 5 years	13	7
5–10 years old	67	18
Over 10 years old	20	75
Relationship to oldest child		
Full sibling	92	91
Half-sibling	8	0
Step-sibling	0	9

Data collection and measures

Information from children's social workers

Children's social workers (CSWs) were interviewed in person at three months about the children's earlier experiences; the reason for separation from siblings who were not placed with them; factors that were influential in making decisions about separation, maintenance or reunion; and plans for contact with separated siblings. The CSWs were re-interviewed by telephone at 12 months and asked for their views on placement progress; to detail the support they had provided; and to describe any particular sibling issues. These telephone interviews used a semi-structured schedule and took about 15–20 minutes to complete.

Information from family placement workers

Family social workers (FSWs) were also interviewed at three and 12 months. The first interview focused on their view of the family's ability to adapt to the placement and the support they anticipated the placement would need. The amount of discussion they had had with resident birth children prior to placement was recorded, as was the extent to which they thought these children would have difficulties in adjusting to their new siblings. The 12 month interview was identical to that conducted with the children's workers.

Information from new parents

The new parents were interviewed at home using a semi-structured interview at three and 12 months after placement. The interview schedule was developed from the schedule used in our previous study of late placements (Quinton et al, 1998) and used well-established investigator-based methods (Brown, 1983). It included demographic information on the family; a modified version of the Isle of Wight schedule (Rutter et al, 1970); and the Parental Account of Children's Symptoms (PACS: Taylor et al, 1986). Information on emotional and behavioural problems was collected for each child in the family.

New measures of sibling relationships were devised. These covered both the dynamics of the group as a whole – including birth children – and also the relationships of each dyad within the group. This section included the important dimensions of sibling relationships highlighted in other research (Furman and Buhrmester, 1985; Dunn and McGuire, 1992) such as the degree of caring and closeness between the children, the extent of co-operation, the amount of rivalry, and the frequency and severity of disputes. It also covered issues known to be important for looked after children such as parentification. Finally, there were questions on contact with birth families, support needs and the parents' assessment of the impact of placement on family members. Parents also completed two questionnaires:

a) A modified version of the *Sibling Relationships Questionnaire* (Furman and Buhrmester, 1985), which measures the degree of warmth and conflict between pairs of children and also assesses the relative power of each child, as indicated by the extent to which one sibling is reported to nurture or dominate the other. These questionnaires were completed at both interview points for all dyads in the family.

b) The *Strengths and Difficulties Questionnaire* (Goodman, 1994) was completed by the parents for all children in the family at 12 months after placement. This instrument provides a series of scores related to problems of conduct, over-activity and emotion along with a pro-social score. It was developed from the Rutter A2 questionnaire but contains positively as well as negatively-worded items. This is felt to make the instruments more comfortable for parents.

Comparison data on sibling relationships

In order to know how the quality of sibling relationships in the study families compared with those in birth families, a comparison group of 100 families was recruited through schools in two areas, one an outer London borough, the other a county in the South East of England. Both were selected to reflect a fairly mixed social class composition similar to that of the new families in the sample. These 100 parents were among those who responded positively to a general invitation via their children's schools to help in the study and are therefore self-selected. From the positive responses, we included those whose family characteristics provided a suitable comparison in terms of age, structure and gender. As with the sample families, those who were caring for adopted or foster children were excluded, as were families who had a disabled child. The comparison families completed telephone interviews, lasting 10–15 minutes, on the interaction between their children as a group and completed the Strengths and Difficulties Questionnaire and the Sibling Relationships Questionnaire by post for two of their children.

We restricted the questionnaire data to one dyad in order to keep the demand on parents to a minimum and thus maximise return rates. This comparison dyad was selected to represent the best available match with the sample dyads. Table A.1 (see Appendix) contains details of the demographic and family characteristics of the sample and comparison groups.

Our primary matching criteria for the comparison group was family size and composition and this match was achieved. However, there were some differences between sample and comparison on other characteristics that warrant some discussion.

First, the comparison group contained a higher proportion of minority ethnic families. This is because the matching was based on the ethnicity of the children rather than the new families. In total, 12 of 72 (12.5 per cent) placements included at least one child of other than white UK origin (all of the children of minority ethnic background in this study were of mixed parentage). The ethnicity data are given for information purposes only; group sizes are too small to warrant any exploration of the data according to ethnicity.

Secondly, the adoptive and foster parents were on average two years older than the comparison parents. Although this difference was statistically significant, it seems unlikely that this difference would affect the ways in which the two groups of parents reported their children's relationships.

Thirdly, it is sometimes suggested that adults who are active in the "caring" professions may be over-represented among those who apply to adopt or foster children. This was not the case in this comparison. While 37 per cent of study families were employed in social work, teaching (of children) or nursing, the same was true of 27 per cent of comparison families, a non-significant difference.

Finally, there were more lone parents in the comparison group. This is not surprising since the study sample in this comparison was restricted to parents who took more than one child and none of the lone parents in the study did so.

Were these differences between the study and comparison groups likely to complicate the comparisons between sibling relationships in the two samples? Spurious findings might arise either if these differences led parents to perceive their children differently or if differences in lone parent or minority ethnic status, age or other factors were strongly related to different patterns of sibling relationships. This seems unlikely. The differences, although statistically significant, are not large. Nevertheless a check was made for possible biases. There were no significant differences *within* the comparison group in the extent to which parents with these characteristics reported conflict, rivalry, warmth or joint activities among their children.

KEY POINTS
Aims, design and methods

- This is a prospective one-year follow up of 72 placements: referrals were received at the point of matching.
- Of 95 appropriate referrals, six disrupted too soon to be interviewed and 17 declined to participate. Of the 23 non-participating cases, 13 (56 per cent) disrupted before the first anniversary of placement. This compares with 10 per cent among participating cases.
- Thirty-two placements were of single children and 40 involved sibling groups. There were 133 placed children and 28 resident birth children.
- Nine of the placements included at least one child of minority ethnic origin. In six of these nine cases the children joined families headed by two white carers.
- Each placement included at least one child between 5 and 11 years old. Two-thirds of the placed children were between 5 and 10 and half were boys.

- Information was collected from participating families and social workers by interviews and questionnaires at 3 and 12 months after placement.
- A community sample was recruited to permit a comparison of sibling relationships in placed samples with those of children growing up in their own families.

3 Sibling networks, contact and placement decisions

In this chapter we consider the extent to which the children had siblings who were not placed with them, that is, we are concerned with those biologically related siblings from whom the children were separated. We call these brothers and sisters "siblings elsewhere". The information on them was provided by the children's social workers at the start of the placement. The interviews were done at their place of work and so they had access to their files to check the details.

Social workers gave us information on how these siblings elsewhere were related to the placed children, where they were living, what the placed children knew of them, the quality of relationship they had, how much contact there had been with them in the past and what was planned for the future. Additional information on sibling contact during the first year of placement was taken from the interviews with the new parents. Where relevant, we also explored with the social workers what lay behind decisions about separation, maintenance or reunion and the extent to which other parties were in agreement with the plan.

Characteristics of the children's siblings elsewhere

In total, we were told of 146 birth siblings who were living apart from the study children. An additional eight siblings had died in infancy. Eighty-seven of these 146 children (59 per cent) were half-siblings to the placed children on the mother's side. Nineteen (13 per cent) were half-siblings on the father's side and 48 (33 per cent) were full siblings to at least one of the placed children. It is possible that some of the placed children also had other half-siblings from their birth fathers' new partnerships, but this information was often unavailable because birth fathers were no longer known to the social workers. One hundred-and-twenty-five of the "siblings elsewhere" were under 17 years old at the time of the study children's placements. We call children under 17 "dependent" siblings. Thus there were 21 older or "independent" ones who had mostly left their family or foster homes. Indeed, their ages went up to 30 and some had children of their own.

In all, 58 of the 72 study *placements* (40 sibling groups and 32 individual children) contained children who had between one and nine siblings living elsewhere. The reader may find the flow chart (Figure 3.1) helpful in understanding the data that follow. The data reflect the birth family composition around the time that the decision to place permanently would have been made.

Figure 3.1

The whereabouts of "siblings elsewhere" for the 72 sample placements

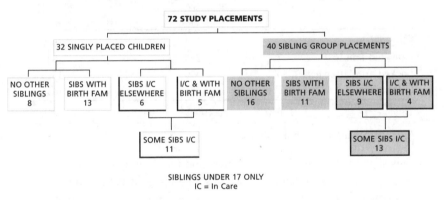

Four of the singly placed children were only children and four had siblings who were very much older. Six of the 16 sibling groups with "no dependent siblings elsewhere" had brothers or sisters who were all independent. The remainder were complete sibling groups placed together.

Where were the "siblings elsewhere" living?

When we examined the whereabouts of the 146 siblings who were elsewhere, we found that 14 per cent had grown up and were living independently at the time of the study placement. Thirty-eight per cent of the siblings (55) were elsewhere in the care system. Forty-two were placed for permanence and 13 were in "short-term" placements, although their return home was not anticipated in the near future. Only 11 (8 per cent) siblings were residing with members of their extended families but, given the parenting experiences of the sample children, a surprising number of their brothers and sisters remained with their birth parents (59/146 (40 per cent)). As is clear from Table 3.1, the siblings of dependent age who remained with the birth or extended family were significantly more likely to be half-, rather than full siblings to the placed children ($\chi^2 = 5.31$, df = 1, p<0.05).

Table 3.1
The whereabouts of siblings according to parentage

	Full siblings $n = 46$	Maternal half-siblings $n = 82$	Paternal half-siblings $n = 18$	Total $n = 146$
Birth parents	37%	39%	55%	40%
Extended family	2%	12%	–	8%
Looked after elsewhere	54%	34%	11%	38%
Independent	7%	14%	33%	14%
Total	100%	100%	100%	100%

Note: Percentages have been rounded up.

This suggests that much of the explanation for children remaining with birth parents was related to changes in family structure but, as a consequence, the children who remained at home were also younger. Sixty-three per cent of the 59 siblings who remained with their birth parents were under five and 16 were under the age of one. The majority of these children were half-siblings to the placed children, mostly on the mother's side (15/16 infants; 13/21 pre-schoolers).

It is clear from Table 3.2 that younger children were more likely to be living with their birth families and that older children of dependent age were significantly more likely to be looked after by local authorities. The fact that the younger siblings remained at home might reflect an improvement in circumstances that allowed some birth parents to parent more adequately. Alternatively, the parents might have been better at bringing up infants but found parenting more difficult as children got older. Most of the social workers reported that progress of these families and their young children was being closely monitored.

Table 3.2
The age distribution of "siblings elsewhere" according to place of residence

Age of sibling	Birth or extended family n = 70	In care n = 55	Independent n = 21	Total n = 146
Under 1	94%	6%		18
1–4 yrs	75%	25%		28
5–10 yrs	32%	68%		32
11–16 yrs	32%	68%		37
17+ yrs	32%		68%	31

($\chi^2 = 30.1$, df = 3, p<.001, excluding those of independent age)

Knowledge of and contact with siblings elsewhere

Table 3.3 illustrates, according to the whereabouts of siblings elsewhere, how many of the siblings were "known" to the placed children, what proportion had stayed in contact in the past and the number for whom future contact plans were in place. Known, in this instance, should be taken to mean that the placed children had at least met and got to know their siblings, although they may not have ever lived together.

Although just over two-thirds of dependent siblings who remained with the birth parents or extended family were known to the placed children, the proportion described by social workers as "well known" was fewer than half (33/70). Face-to-face contact had been maintained prior to this placement with only 24 of these siblings and there were plans for contact to continue with only 14 of them.

As is clear from Table 3.3, siblings who were living elsewhere in the care system were somewhat more likely to be known by the placed children and significantly more likely to have had face-to-face contact with them in the past and for this to be expected in the future. However, it is striking that there was no plan to maintain contact with 40 per cent of "looked after" siblings. Indeed, there was a substantial reduction in anticipated contact associated with the permanent placement for siblings living with birth family and those in care elsewhere.

Three factors may explain the extent of contact with siblings who remain with the birth family. Firstly, sibling contact is likely to be heavily

35

Table 3.3

The proportion of siblings maintaining face-to-face contact with the placed children according to place of residence

	Whereabouts of siblings elsewhere				
	Birth family n = 59	Extended family n = 11	Indep- endent n = 21	In care n = 55	significance of group differences
Known to the placed children	68%	82%	67%	89%	$\chi^2 = 8.6$, df = 3, p<.05
Contact in past	34%	36%	57%	78%	$\chi^2 = 24.0$, df = 3, p<.001
Contact in future	17%	36%	43%	60%	$\chi^2 = 20.6$, df = 3, p<.001

influenced by whether there is to be continuing contact with birth parents. Secondly, the siblings who were at home with birth parents were less likely to be full siblings. Thirdly, many of them were very young and likely to have been born subsequent to the placed children leaving their families of origin. These latter two factors may also have had some bearing on practitioners' considerations of the importance of continuing contact. If this is the case, it suggests that sibling contact may be decided on the basis of the current significance of the relationship rather than its possible future importance.

Relationships between placed children and siblings elsewhere

In trying to determine what led to plans for contact, we examined the relationships that each of these siblings had with the placed children. For the most part, the social workers were able to draw on a reasonable familiarity with the case and the views of the children's carers in order to describe the relationships between children. Therefore, although these ratings were not based on detailed descriptions or observations of relationships, they were sufficient to explore whether the relationship between children had a bearing on continuing contact or whether it was more dependent on other factors.

Regardless of whether the siblings were living with the birth family or were elsewhere in care, the social workers felt that relationships were poor with only about one-sixth of them. Interestingly, there were no reports of poor relationships between independent siblings and placed children. Somewhat surprisingly, the quality of the relationships was not associated with whether contact had been maintained in the past, whereas plans for contact with dependent siblings were significantly related to the quality of the relationship. The better the relationship with the sibling, the more likely were plans for future contact. This was true regardless of whether the children were in care or living with their birth families. Despite this trend, it was interesting to note that there were seven siblings who were looked after elsewhere with whom contact was to continue despite a poor relationship between the children. This may be a reflection of the social workers' desire to see placed children retain some links with their family of origin with an eye to their future rather than their current needs where children were separated within the care system.

Sibling contact from a placement perspective
It is important to consider sibling contact from the perspective of placements as well as from that of individual children. For example, contact plans are likely to apply to sibling groups as a whole rather than to individual children and thus the figures based on children may reflect concentrations of problems in a few cases rather than general tendencies across the whole sample.

Examining the data from this perspective, we found that definite plans for face-to-face contact with siblings had been made in only 29 of the 58 placements where the children had siblings elsewhere (including the 10 cases where siblings were older). There were two cases in which the children were to have some postal contact with their siblings but no meetings. There were also eight cases where the social worker was hoping to arrange some form of sibling contact. In the great majority of cases where face-to-face contact had been planned (83 per cent), the level of that contact was judged by the social worker to be sufficient to meet the needs of the children although it rarely entailed contact with all possible siblings. For the remaining five cases, social workers felt the level of contact to be insufficient and were concerned that lack of contact may lead to difficulties for the children.

Social workers were also concerned that the lack of contact might be a cause of difficulty for 11 of the 29 cases where no contact had been arranged. This scenario sometimes occurred when all of the siblings remained with the birth family and the birth parents were refusing any contact with the placed child. In this circumstance, arranging contact would have been very difficult despite the social workers' recognition of potential difficulties. While singly placed children were no more likely than others to have contact arrangements with their siblings, there was a tendency for social workers to feel that lack of sibling contact would be potentially more problematic for singletons ($\chi^2 = 6.0$, $df = 2$; $p<0.05$).

Contact with siblings during the first year of permanent placement
In total, 28 of the 32 singly placed and 74 of the 101 jointly placed children were recorded as having siblings who were living elsewhere. Of these, 12 month data concerning contact were only available for 20 and 56 respectively. In the main, missing data were accounted for by parental withdrawal from the study or placement disruption (16 children) although there were also 13 children in seven placements for whom the information was simply not known. These tended to be placements where the siblings were not known to the placed children and the siblings themselves were either very much older or very much younger.

In the course of discussing sibling contact with new families, we asked about the feelings that the placed children showed towards their brothers and sisters who were living elsewhere. The responses are broadly grouped in Table 3.5. Children placed with siblings were far more likely than those placed alone to show no feelings at all toward their siblings elsewhere (48 per cent as opposed to 20 per cent). However, it is striking that a substantial proportion of both singly (45 per cent) and jointly placed children (31 per cent) either harboured negative feelings, worries and concerns or were described as actively missing their brothers and sisters. It was encouraging that plans for contact were in place for the majority of this latter group.

Feelings of anger or fear tended to be towards siblings who were in care and of a similar age or older. Concern and confusion tended to be focused on younger siblings who remained with the birth family. It was not unusual for interviewers to hear tales of the eldest child of a placed group, who had taken the burden of raising the younger ones, worrying about how their birth mother was managing later born children.

Table 3.5
Parent reports of children's feelings towards siblings during the first year of placement

Feelings shown, according to parents	Singly placed n = 20	Jointly placed n = 56
None at all	20%	48%
Anger or fear	10%	7%
Concern or confusion	15%	9%
Affection, misses sibling/s	20%	14%
Affection, accepts separation	35%	21%

Confusion could arise when children were unable to understand why they had been removed when their parent/s were continuing to care for the younger ones. This group, although small in number, was least likely to be in contact. While contact in this situation might have provided much needed reassurance for some placed children, it would clearly need careful management, since it is also possible that confusion may be exacerbated by seeing parents coping successfully with other children.

For the most part, new parents' understanding of a plan for contact was in line with the expectations of social workers, although they tended to interpret social workers' discussions of the possibility of contact as a plan. Figures 3.2a and 3.2b present the extent to which direct sibling contact had occurred by the end of the year from the new parents' understanding of the plans. The group numbers vary, firstly because only those cases with siblings who took part in the one-year interview are included. Additionally, the *extent* of contact for jointly placed children is presented as a proportion of sibling group placements, since all contact arrangements were made for the group as a whole. The *effect* of the contact for these children is dealt with on an individual basis, since one child in a group may respond very differently from another. Because of the potential importance of knowing separated siblings later in life, we have included cases where the only possibility of contact was with independent siblings, although we acknowledge that social workers may have less influence in planning in these circumstances. In fact the pattern of contact remains similar whether or not these young adults are included. These data are illustrated in Figures 3.3a and 3.3b.

As is clear from the charts, singly placed children were more likely than sibling groups to have had face-to-face contact with siblings elsewhere during the year, although not significantly so. In only one singleton placement had there been a contact plan that had not materialised, whereas planned contact had not happened in four sibling group placements.

Figures 3.2a and 3.2b
The extent of sibling contact during the year for singly and jointly placed children

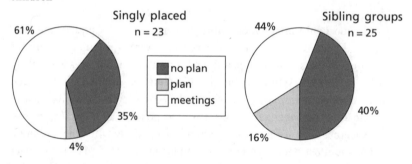

Figures 3.3a and 3.3b
The effect of sibling contact during the year for singly and jointly placed children

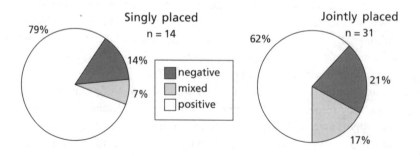

SIBLING NETWORKS, CONTACT AND PLACEMENT DECISIONS

On the whole, sibling contact was viewed positively for both groups (see Figures 3.3a and 3.3b), although a slightly higher proportion of new parents of jointly placed children reported that contact with siblings had a mixed or negative effect. In both groups the proportion of families reporting mixed or negative effects reduced over the year as everyone adjusted to the experience. More lasting negative parental assessments of contact were associated with the exposure of the children to "mixed messages" or undesirable lifestyles or where the children were actually frightened of their siblings.

The case of Sara and Karl provides an example of the former circumstance. They were placed together for long-term foster care when they were 14 and 10 years old. They had three older siblings who were living independently at the time of the study and a younger brother and sister who were placed elsewhere in long-term foster care. The placement was made with regular contact with the younger siblings and the children would also go out for periods with their older siblings. The new parents' anxieties about the contact concerned details about the lifestyles of the young adults that were conveyed to the children. For example, their older sister was in a violent relationship with a man but stressed to Sara and Karl that it was 'the only way a girl could get nice jewellery and clothes'. Another was believed to be a prostitute. Set against the values of the foster family who were trying to encourage behaviour appropriate to the children's ages, the effect for the children was one of confusion. One of the siblings also breached a confidentiality agreement and passed the carer's home phone number to the birth parents, which then resulted in abusive phone calls. In such circumstances it is not surprising that, despite being strongly positive in principle, the carers harboured anxieties about the impact of some of the sibling contact on the children. Other adoptive parents spoke about the impact of a contact meeting between the child placed with them and his older sister. Both children had been sexually abused. Not all the details of the abuse were known, but the adopters felt that the meeting not only brought back the memories of the abuse but that the child also found his sister very frightening.

The major obstacle to sibling contact tended to be negotiating with the carers of the "other" siblings, as there were examples of resistance from both custodial birth parents and other adopters. The majority of

41

new parents were very open to facilitating contact, although practicalities could be awkward when many children, different placements or long distances were involved.

Placement decisions

Aside from the decision to remove children from their parents, decisions about separating or maintaining siblings in placement must be one of the most taxing demands on child care social workers. We were interested to explore what patterns of separation and reunion were to be found in the children's histories, the reasons that lay behind past decisions and the factors that influenced the practitioners in their plans for the perm- anent placement.

Most of the children were at least five years old at the time of the study and many had been looked after by the local authority for some years. As a group they had complex histories of moves into, out of, and within the care system and some of the children had elaborate sibling networks. In order to explore the way in which decisions about splitting or maintaining sibling groups had been made in the past, we had first to define a sample of children for whom such decisions were possible or relevant. For this reason children with no siblings elsewhere in the care system were excluded from this analysis. We also excluded children whose siblings were all considerably older, given that deci- sions about placement together would probably not have been relevant. For example, there were some children whose siblings were in care but approaching independence at the time of their birth.

When it came to making plans for the permanent placement, decisions that had been taken some time previously were not often reversed and the majority of the study placements represented a continuation of previous placement constellations. Two of the singly placed children had been in their previous placement together with a sibling and the decision had been taken to separate them when planning their permanent placements. Six of the sibling group placements represented a degree of reunion for the children involved. There had also been considerable discussion about whether a further eight sibling groups were best placed together although the eventual decision had been to maintain the status quo.

Reasons for separation and reunion possibilities for separated children

As illustrated in Figure 3.1, there was a total of 13 sibling groups and 11 singly placed children who had at least one sibling elsewhere in the care system. Between them these children had 55 "siblings elsewhere". The two most common explanations given by the social workers for the children not being placed together were either that the children entered care at different times (24/55), or that at least one of the children had specific needs that dictated separate placement (27/55). In only one case did the placed children have siblings who were placed separately purely because of placement availability (3 of 55 "siblings elsewhere") and in one case the separation had been due to the wishes of the study child.

All but one of the 11 singly placed children had been with one or more of their siblings at some point while in care. Only two of these children had been separated for this placement and on average these children had been on their own in foster care for over two years (mean 25.27; sd = 15.59; range 0–53 months). Considerable thought had usually been applied to the initial separation of the children and in seven of the nine cases of longstanding separation, some consideration had been given to the possibility of reunion when planning the permanent placement.

In contrast, the 13 sibling groups who had siblings elsewhere in the care system tended to have been together for most of their time in care. In only one case had a group ever been placed with other siblings as well. Over half the existing separations were ascribed to the needs of the children but the others had occurred as a result of circumstantial factors, such as different times of entry to care or availability of placements. Consideration of reunion for these splintered sibling groups had occurred in six of the 13 cases. At first glance this suggests that much less attention was given to the circumstances of some sibling groups. However, a closer look at the characteristics of the children and the reasons for separation revealed a somewhat different picture. These reasons are summarised in Table 3.6 and are discussed in more detail below.

Table 3.6
Reason for separations from siblings

	Sibling groups	Singletons	Total
A child's needs	7	5	16
Relationship between siblings	–	4	–
Reception dates different	5	1	6
Placement availability	1	–	1
A child's wishes	–	1	1
Total	13	11	24

Factors associated with separate placement
When separations had arisen because of behavioural difficulties in the children or because of difficulties in their relationships, the separations were usually seen as a response to the children's needs. However, these difficulties could also feed into the decision to separate if they were thought to reduce the chance of finding a family. Even if a family could be found there was concern that a particularly difficult child would increase the risk of disruption. However, these views were clearly not applied consistently. There were sibling groups in the study who demonstrated a good deal of conflict and bad feeling towards each other, and groups containing children showing considerable behavioural difficulties. We were not able to identify any factors that discriminated between those with problematic behaviour or relationships who were separated and those who remained together. It is possible that factors like the perceived tolerance of carers or social workers' commitment to maintaining sibling ties came into play.

We examined a number of other factors that might have been influential in the decision to split or reunite sibling groups, but no clear patterns were discernible. For example, the possibility of finding a family able to accommodate some of the larger sibling groups might have been problematic. However, both single and sibling group placements had between one and six siblings looked after elsewhere and the extent to which reunion was discussed for this placement was not associated with the number of siblings elsewhere for either single or sibling group placements.

Neither the extent to which the children knew siblings elsewhere nor the quality of relationship between them was associated with consideration of reunion. Indeed, contrary to what might be expected, a consideration of reunion was more likely when past separation had been due to children's needs than when the reason had been different dates of admission to care or placement availability. This may have arisen because the age gap between placed and separated children was larger when separation was due to these more practical factors. Although the age differences were not significant, they may have discouraged reunion in some cases.

The possibility of reunion was more likely to be considered for both sibling groups and singly placed children when siblings elsewhere were full siblings to those placed ($\chi^2 = 6.1$, df = 1, p<0.05). However, one-quarter of the study sibling groups included at least some half-siblings, suggesting that this relationship did not necessarily exclude the possibility of joint placement. Among the study sibling groups in particular there was a tendency for half-siblings looked after elsewhere to differ substantially in age from sample children.

Although numbers are too small to allow statistical tests, it seemed that a combination of age differences and the biological relationship between children may explain why reunion was not considered for some of the splintered sibling groups in the study. This is the same combination of factors we highlighted earlier as being associated with a lack of sibling contact.

The singly placed children in the sample were almost always separated on the basis of perceived individual needs but we were somewhat surprised to find that, in half of the six cases of splintering of sibling groups that were due to practicalities of admission, the placed children had only one other sibling in care. This seems to be explained by the fact that there were substantial age differences and long gaps between admission dates in these cases. Thus, some of these separated children may have been well settled in their own placement at the time the sample children entered care.

The case of Jamie and Ryan illustrates this to an extent. These two boys, who were full siblings, were six and three years old at placement. They were the youngest children from a large sibling group: four on their mother's side and four on their father's side, although only two of the siblings were also looked after. These last two children were half-siblings to Jamie and Ryan and they were 15 and 12 years old at the time that Jamie and Ryan moved to their new family. They had entered care and been placed together around four months earlier than the two study children but had never been placed with them. There had been fleeting thoughts of placing them with their older sisters, but these were quickly dismissed because of the level of difficulties the girls were having. The social worker in this case reported that there had been a time when they thought about splitting Jamie and Ryan, because there were worries that Ryan might be easier for new carers to engage with and Jamie might miss out as a result. Although these possibilities were discussed in meetings, there had been no actual assessment. The children ended up being placed together because the behaviour of the elder of the two improved a little, reducing the worries about him not being as "accept-able" as the younger child. There had initially been plans for there to be contact between the separated siblings; however, these plans had floundered before placement because of new disclosures about sexual abuse in the family and who might have been affected by it. At the time of the first interview, the social worker was hoping that it might be possible to get the contact plans back on track; however, the children did not see their brothers and sisters during the first year of placement.

Bearing in mind that most of the sibling groups in our sample did not have siblings elsewhere in the care system, it seems that social workers were for the most part operating within the guidance that encourages maintenance of sibling groups. Where separation occurred, it usually resulted from the social workers' assessment of the needs of individual children. The exceptions were those cases in which the separated siblings were markedly different in age and had only one birth parent in common with the placed children.

Factors influencing the social work decisions
There are a number of pressures on social workers when faced with the dilemma of how to place a group of related children all of whom are in care. They must try to balance the competing needs of the children themselves, their parents, the views of others, and the likelihood of

finding a placement where large groups of possibly difficult children can be accommodated. Social workers were asked about the extent to which consideration had been given to each of a number of factors when making the decision about the permanent placement. These questions were asked for any placement where there was an element of choice. All sibling placements were included in this analysis since splitting was potentially possible and indeed, for some, reunion may also have been feasible. All singleton placements were included if there were other siblings in the care system.

Figures 3.4 and 3.5
Influential factors in the decision making process for sibling groups and singly placed children

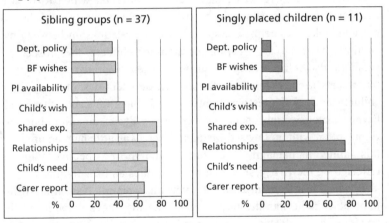

When the social workers were considering splitting, splintering or reunion, they tended to be most influenced by the relationships between the children and the children's individual needs. Shared history and other carers' accounts of how the children were together were also important factors for most social workers. The expressed wishes of the children were considered important in just under half of the cases. The wishes of the birth family and placement availability were prime factors in only one-third of cases (see Figures 3.4 and 3.5).

There was a tendency for individual needs and previous carer reports to be more prominent for singleton placements (χ^2 = 4.8 and 5.9 respectively, df = 1, p<.05 in both cases). To some extent at least this is perhaps a reflection of the fact that in a few cases carers were reporting difficulties with sibling group placements that social workers were not entirely convinced about. For example, a group of boys aged between five and eight at placement had been in care, placed together, for three-and-a-half years. When the social worker took over the case, the foster carers were reporting significant difficulties in the interaction between the children, and on this basis were recommending separation for the permanent placement. Other professionals who had knowledge of the case also shared these views. However, the new social worker felt that the children, despite their individual needs, were very supportive towards each other and there was insufficient evidence on which to base a decision to separate. Although she articulated this view strongly she did not undertake a systematic assessment of the relationship between the children. After a year of caring for the three children, the prospective adopters also felt that they should have been separated and adoptive placements secured for them earlier. The adopters described all three children as very aggressive, showing no feelings for each other at all beyond jealousy. Time spent together rapidly degenerated into physical fights, often with improvised weapons. There was little help on offer for this family in managing the conflict and the prospective adopters reflected on the first year as one of difficulties and frustrations.

It is not clear from the case notes why this worker felt so strongly that joint placement was the best choice. She may have disbelieved the previous carers, dismissed the importance of conflict between children or felt the children might behave differently with different carers. We did not have a measure of how strongly practitioners felt with regard to maintenance of sibling groups, but it is possible that for some, such views may be strongly held and may on occasion override other considerations. One worker did articulate her own position: 'My own personal view is that if we can, we should be placing children together. However, I recognise that this view could influence my decision and I feel sure that if children were saying otherwise, I would be able to listen.' Implicit in this statement is a need, whenever views are strongly held, to be sure that decisions are based on objective and systematic information, gleaned from as many sources as possible.

The most important factors mentioned by social workers placing sibling groups appeared to be shared experience and the relationships between the children, although these were not ignored by the workers who eventually chose to place a child alone. Social workers tended to view joint placement for children who had shared experience in the past as a positive and potentially protective feature. They thought it allowed children to share and compare memories and to keep images of the past intact and accurate. This was not, however, always the case. On occasion, new parents on carers reported on one child's need to "rewrite" their history for their own reasons and this could lead to substantial disagreement and upset between siblings.

The relationship between children was seen as important for both joint and singleton placements although for the opposite reasons. Where children were to be placed separately, it was usually the case that relationships between them were strained, whereas many of the joint placements were made because the children supported and relied upon each other. In many cases of joint placement there was perhaps little for workers to agonise about with regard to the best placement option for the children. A number of the sibling groups had been together through-out their time in care and their relationships were unremarkable. How-ever, there were some circumstances in which it was very difficult for workers to make the eventual decision about joint or separate placement. One social worker's assessment of the seven and eight-year-old boys in her care was that, although they had some positive feelings for each other, their relationship was largely characterised by conflict and both showed a good deal of very difficult behaviour. She had almost come to the conclusion that their interests would best be served by seeking separate placements. But on one occasion, when she was returning with them in her car, the conversation touched on something to do with moving families. As this was said she saw, in her rear view mirror, the children reach for each other and hold hands on the back seat. Her view changed at that moment and was subsequently endorsed by a full assessment and by other professionals involved with the children. The first year of placement did indeed prove to be a struggle for the prospective adopters: the children needed extensive therapeutic help for their behaviour problems and their relationship continued to be fraught. However, the new parents' evaluation of the year as a whole was positive. Perhaps the big difference between this case example and the previous one of the three boys is that the social worker in this case, because she had been considering separation, recognised that the adopters might face difficulties with the behaviour and the relationships of the children. The possibilities had been discussed with the family prior to placement and support was forthcoming.

Overall, it seems that in most cases the factors driving workers' choices were centred on their perception of the welfare of the children at the time. Practical and policy factors were taken into consideration in fewer cases.

Degree of multi-party agreement about placement plans

In most cases other involved parties agreed with the plans pursued by the social workers regarding the separation or maintenance of siblings. In only 13 of 48 possible cases was there any dissent at all: five cases where previous carers disagreed with the decision, three cases where birth parents felt differently and three where other professionals felt the chosen path was not the best option. In one case a mixture of other parties disagreed with the key worker's plans and there was one case in which one of the placed children was unhappy about being placed as part of a sibling group.

The disagreement mostly concerned the maintenance of sibling groups. As illustrated earlier, previous carers sometimes suggested that children whose interaction was especially characterised by conflict may be better placed separately. However, as revealed in Figure 3.6, for the most part the first year of placement seemed to be going well even where there had been opposition to the plans. (See Chapter 5 for a discussion of outcomes and outcome measures.)

Figure 3.6

New parents' evaluation of placement at a year according to agreement with the placement plan

%

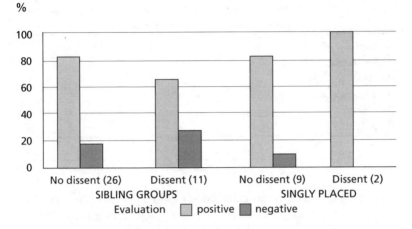

The use of formal assessments of sibling relationships
===

The use of formal assessments of sibling relationships

We looked at the extent to which formal assessment procedures had been used to confirm or assist the advisability of placement plans. Although there is as yet no routinely used structure to guide assessment of sibling relationships, a number of approaches have been proposed in the literature (see for example DoH, 1991; Lord and Borthwick, 2001, forthcoming) and some local authorities have developed their own checklists for reference when deciding about placement options.

On the whole we found that there was relatively little use of any sort of structured procedure informing social workers' decisions in this regard. It was more likely that an assessment was conducted when the decision was to place a child alone. As shown in Table 3.7, social workers reported thorough assessments for just over half of the children who were placed alone and apart from their siblings. In contrast, of the 13 sibling groups where there was a possibility of reunion with other brothers or sisters, assessment had only occurred in two cases. Assessments were carried out to establish that continued placement together was the best option for one-third of jointly placed sibling groups.

Table 3.7
Type of sibling assessment according to singleton or sibling group placement

	Sibling groups Continue together	Sibling groups Potential reunion	Singletons	Total
No formal assessment	19	11	5	35
By child/ren's SW	4	2	1	7
By appointed SW	2	–	1	3
By therapist	1	–	1	2
By psychiatrist	1	–	3	4
Total	27	13	11	51

One case stood out as a particularly noteworthy example of good practice. A group of four children, three girls and a boy, were placed for long-term fostering separately from their older brother and sister. In their temporary foster placements, the eldest two were placed in one foster home, the middle two in another and youngest two in another. In trying to reach decisions about the permanent placements, three experienced workers from a family placement unit worked together on how the children should best be placed for permanence. The assessment involved a mixture of joint and individual sessions over a period of five weeks.

One of the social workers described the period of work in this way. 'We started by doing five structured sessions with all the children. The reason for doing this is that everybody who had known the children had a different view about the groupings, or "not groupings" as it were, that the children should be placed in. We felt we needed to hear what the children were saying about it. I think they had been placed in their bridging placements as a matter of convenience rather than how they wanted to be placed. We came to the decision that we had more of a chance of placing the four younger children in a family placement. One of the older children might possibly have been placed with them too, but he was 14 and happy with his foster family who were prepared to keep him long term. The younger children felt that, much as they enjoyed being with him and he with them, they felt he was so happy in his placement that as long as they could all see each other it was right that he should stay. Even the youngest was saying his brother should stay because he was happy.' Once the decision was made, substantial direct work continued, with each social worker seeing two children to help them understand what had happened in the past and to prepare them for the new placement. The new placement was arranged with regular contact planned but to be negotiated with the two sets of carers. There had already been two contact meetings by the time the three-month interview was due.

Mark and Simon were also the youngest of a larger sibling group of six, all placed in pairs. However, there was a difference of only around 18 months between each of the six children. All six children had at some point lived together, they knew each other well, and all were in need of long-term care at the time of placement. In this case, the social worker responsible for their care said: 'They are close in age, but I don't really know why they have been kept together'. The social worker we were talking to was new to the case and did not know the boys; nevertheless, there was nothing on the file to suggest that any systematic assessment had been conducted about the possibilities of reuniting some of the siblings in their permanent placement. This case runs counter to our overall findings about splintering of sibling groups, which more usually conformed to the pattern outlined in the previous example, but it illustrates to some extent the problems that can occur with rapid staff change. In the few months that elapsed between these children being referred to the study and our trying to conduct the first interviews, there had been three changes of social worker allocated to these boys and their siblings (we do not know how many social workers they had had altogether). Neither the children nor their new family had seen or heard from a children's worker since placement. Given the organisational difficulties associated with the rapid staff turnover, it is not surprising to learn that although a plan for sibling contact between these separated children was made, a contact arrangement was not realised in the course of the year.

While the rates of assessment were higher for those who were to be placed singly, given the presumed importance of keeping siblings together, it remains of concern that for nearly half of these children no *systematic* consideration was given to the possibility of reunion when permanent plans were being made. In fact, there was no significant difference in the proportion of poor outcomes according to whether or not there had been a formal assessment, but there were differences in the reasons for the poor outcomes. Two of 14 cases in which there had been a full assessment were rated unstable at one year, but the reasons for this were concerned more with the way the children were settling into the family than with the children's relationships with each other. Of the six cases of poor outcome where there had been no formal assessment, at least four cases showed high levels of friction between the children which influenced, at least to an extent, the parents' evaluations of the placement.

We would argue that assessments with regard to the relationships between related children and their degree of reliance on each other ought to be conducted routinely, regardless of where they are currently living. An assessment can be much more than purely a justification for separation, it can inform practitioners, current carers, prospective families and even birth families about potential strengths and difficulties and the relative importance of a sibling in a child's life.

Overview

This chapter has been concerned with the siblings "placed elsewhere". In a large majority of the study placements (80 per cent) there was at least one sibling living elsewhere. Two-thirds of these were half-siblings. Just over one-third were in the care system and these were more likely to be known by and to have contact with the study children than those not looked after. There were no plans for contact in a substantial number of cases. In some cases, contact between siblings was thought to be desirable by social workers but was not permitted by the birth parents. New parents were generally happy to facilitate contact. Where sibling contact had been planned, it usually occurred during the course of the first year of placement and for the most part parents reported positive effects, particularly in the case of singly placed children. Where parents were uneasy about the contact it was most commonly due to poor relationships between the children or the study children's feelings towards their siblings.

Although placement availability had occasionally figured in social workers' decisions to separate siblings in the past, the commonest reasons were that the dates of reception into care differed or that separation was based on the children's needs. Where reception dates were given as a reason for separation, we found that the separated children usually differed substantially in age and were frequently half-siblings to those placed. Separations due to individual needs usually resulted from the difficult behaviour of one or more siblings or problems with the relationship between them.

Social workers discussed how these factors discouraged joint placement because of the increased likelihood of the difficulties leading to disruption and the possible negative effects on the children themselves. It is clear that the need to secure permanency was, at times, competing with the aim of maintaining siblings together. Undoubtedly much more needs to be known about the longer-term impact of separation for children in order that the most appropriate decisions can be made. This is especially the case where the choice is between separation and joint placement where relationships are poor. Additionally, there is a very obvious requirement to focus attention on helping children overcome the problems of behaviour or poor relationships, which may otherwise lead to their being parted.

Although a good deal of thought had been given to the way in which children were to be placed, we found that the use of a formal assessment of sibling relationships was rare. A structured method of investigating relationships between children may be a valuable tool for social workers. Such a technique would be helpful not just to help in decisions about separating children, but also in the task of preparing and supporting carers and children.

KEY POINTS
Sibling networks, contact and
placement decisions

- In 80 per cent of the sample placements, at least one sibling was living elsewhere.
- Contact was more likely with another child in the care system than with a child living in the birth family.
- New parents were generally happy to facilitate contact; however, negative parental assessments of contact were associated with the exposure of the children to mixed messages from birth siblings or their undesirable lifestyles or where the children were actually frightened of their siblings.
- Children living with some of their siblings were less likely to show feelings for siblings elsewhere compared with children placed alone.
- In this sample, separation of siblings when children were to be placed alone was usually a response to the social worker's assessment of the needs of individual children. For some splintered sibling groups there seemed less consideration given but this was usually when there were very large age gaps and different parentage between the placed group and other siblings.
- Placement plans with regard to maintenance together or separation of siblings were not always agreed by all those involved with the children and previous carers sometimes recommended splitting on the basis of conflicted sibling relationships. However, placements which took place despite dissent were no more likely to proceed poorly than those in which all parties agreed.
- There was scope for much more structured assessment on which to base placement decisions – however, such assessment as had been conducted was not associated with markedly better outcome.

4 The children's earlier experiences

Experiences in the birth family

Apart from two single children who were looked after because their birth parents had died, all of the children in this study were placed in permanent substitute families because their birth parents were considered not able to care for them adequately. In these circumstances, a picture of marked family and parenting difficulties in the children's family backgrounds is hardly a surprise (Figure 4.1). Overt discord and violence marked over half of the parental relationships and this was especially common in the sibling group placements. These domestic problems occurred in a context of hardship, poor living conditions and poverty. In about one-third of cases, the birth families had experienced periods of frequent house moves and a pattern of multiple caregivers was a feature in about half the cases. As the previous chapter showed, family breakdown and reconstitution was common and many children were part of families with step- and half-siblings. These factors were not necessarily present throughout the children's entire time with their birth families, but were of significance at least some of the time.

As a consequence of unstable parental partnerships, data on birth fathers were often missing. Many of the birth fathers had not been involved with the children's lives for many years, and data relied on the level of detail in the records or the chance that the social worker had known the families for a long time. There were six cases in which the children's birth father was known to have died and four cases where the birth mother had died prior to the children's current placement.

Nearly a third of birth mothers (31 per cent) and 15 per cent of fathers had had treatment for psychiatric illness. Social work records often underestimate the level of clinically significant psychiatric problems and personality disorder among fathers (Quinton and Rutter, 1984). Birth mothers had had criminal convictions in only 13 per cent of cases, almost all for minor offences, but convictions were more common among birth fathers, 16 per cent of whom had been convicted of minor or

Figure 4.1
The frequency of adverse family experiences for singletons and sibling groups

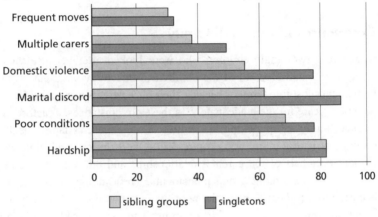

□ sibling groups   ■ singletons

Table 4.1
The quality of care offered by birth parents

	Physical care birth mother	Physical care birth father	Psycho-social care birth mother	Psycho-social care birth father
Poor	41 (59%)	27 (53%)	56 (77%)	38 (76%)
Mixed	12 (17%)	6 (12%)	8 (11%)	8 (16%)
Fair or good	17 (24%)	18 (34%)	7 (9%)	4 (8%)
Total	70	51	71	50

isolated incidents while 15 per cent were described as serious or persistent offenders.

Details concerning parenting were available for 71 birth mothers (one child had never lived with his birth mother) and for 50 birth fathers. Poor levels of physical care were recorded for over half of the birth mothers and fathers. The situation was even more marked when psychological and social aspects of parenting were considered. Over three-quarters of both mothers and fathers showed poor psycho-social care of the children and this was recorded as fair or good for under 10 per cent of parents (Table 4.1).

Factors precipitating reception into care
The most common reasons underlying the children's initial separation from their birth family homes were emotional abuse (loosely defined), neglect and not coping. These three factors were mentioned as a cause for concern in two-thirds of cases, whereas physical or sexual abuse was mentioned in 35 per cent of cases and abandonment in 10 per cent. In around two-thirds of cases, care proceedings were precipitated by concerns about failure to cope with the parenting task, neglect and emotional abuse but with no concrete evidence of either physical or sexual abuse.

Figure 4.2
Frequency of concerns precipitating admission to care (n = 72)

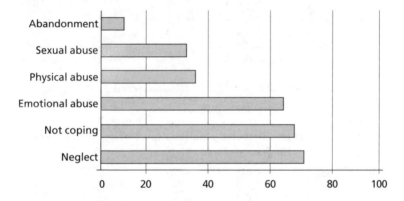

Abuse history
The incidents leading to care proceedings, as outlined above, were of course recorded on a case-by-case basis; however, it was also necessary to understand a little about each child's individual experience of parenting and care with the birth family. We found that, considered in this way, the majority of the 133 children had experienced abusive parenting, with neglect and emotional abuse, perhaps predictably, being the most common (see Figures 4.3 and 4.4). The categories are not mutually

exclusive and most of the children would have experienced more than one type of maltreatment. For the most part the patterns of abuse were similar for single and sibling group placements. The exception to this was scapegoating or rejection by birth parents, which occurred for 31 per cent of children placed singly, but was recorded for only 15 per cent of jointly placed children.

Figure 4.3
The proportion of singly placed children experiencing different types of maltreatment (n = 32 singly placed children)

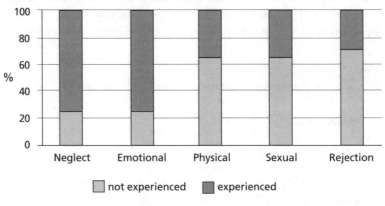

Figure 4.4
The proportion of jointly placed children experiencing different types of maltreatment (n = 101 jointly placed children)

As is clear from the figures (4.3 and 4.4), the most frequently occurring types of abuse were neglect and emotional abuse. "Emotional abuse" did not simply reflect particularly hostile parenting, but included other behaviours that were thought to be damaging to the psychosocial development of the child. In some cases this was associated with mental disorder, which meant that a parent was unable to provide appropriate and consistent parenting – an unintentional but nonetheless significant form of adverse parenting. Physical and sexual abuse were less common but were still experienced by over one-third of the children.

Our previous study showed that scapegoating and rejection were particularly important types of emotional abuse. A rejected or scape-goated child was often the only child from a family who was in care, but even among the sibling groups there were a number of children whom social workers described as having been singled out from siblings and subjected to marked emotionally hostile parenting. The experiences of these rejected children included such features as being dressed differently from siblings, being prevented from joining in with family activities, being blamed for accidents or the wrongdoing of other children, and in extreme cases some children were physically abandoned to the care of social services.

Most abusive parenting was experienced while the children were living with their birth parents, but there were a small number of cases (15 children from 10 families) where the care system had not served them well and abuse had occurred in foster homes. For nine of these 15 children, the abusers were the foster carers themselves, the remaining six children were abused by another child within the home. Abuse by another child involved sexual abuse in five cases and physical abuse in the other. Abuse at the hands of foster carers tended to be emotional maltreatment, although it should be noted that this is not reflected in the figures given for scapegoating or rejection by birth parents as outlined above.

Degree of shared experience of maltreatment
We were interested in establishing the extent to which neglectful or abusive parenting had been experienced by all of the children in the 40 sibling groups. It was clear that the extent of common treatment

depended on the size of the groups. Children in two placements had been treated in broadly similar ways in 65 per cent of cases whereas this was true for only 35 per cent of larger groups. Indeed, there were eight groups in which one child had been favoured by the birth parents which usually meant much less in the way of hostile experiences. These favoured children were not necessarily the youngest of the family. Neglect and emotionally abusive parenting were usually experienced by all of the children but sexual and physical abuse were more likely to be directed more selectively, particularly in larger families. Rejection usually applied to only one child within a sibling group, but in three cases all the placed children had been rejected while other siblings of the same family had not. The numbers involved here were far too small to warrant statistical analyses but nevertheless it is worth noting that similar early experiences should not be assumed, especially for groups of three or more children.

Moves into, out of, and within the care system

For all 133 children, the average age at first admission to care was four, (range 1 month to just over 11 years; standard deviation 2.5 years). The children spent an average of 3 years 8 months in care (range: 5 months to 11 years; s.d. 2 years) and were placed in the study placements at an average age of seven-and-a-half (range: 34 months to 14 years). There were no differences between singly and jointly placed children in any of these measures.

On average, the children had experienced four moves within the care system, but there was a wide range from one to an alarming 26 changes of placement. Fifty-four children returned home at some point following their reception into care: on average they did so twice, although the range was from one to nine times. There was a tendency for singly placed children to have experienced more moves but not significantly so. Of the 40 sibling groups, just over 70 per cent had entered care together and moved together throughout their care history. In the remaining 30 per cent of cases, the older children had experienced more moves and more returns home. This suggested that concern about the family's ability to cope had been long-standing, perhaps preceding the birth of some of the younger children, and that the final decision to remove the children and seek permanence had been made after substantial attempts to support the family.

Despite the wide range in the number of moves the children had experienced and the number of times they had returned home, we could identify no relationship between these placement differences and outcome. We would not wish to imply that multiple moves within care are without consequences, simply that the relationship is likely to be complex. A count of the number of moves that children have experienced is unlikely to be a good indicator of whether children will settle into placements, without taking into account the reason for their moves and their character.

The behaviour of previous carers in preparing children for permanence

The contribution of previous carers is likely to be influential in getting the children ready to move on and in helping them with the transition. Seventy-eight "previous carers" were involved (this is 78 rather than 72 because some placements involved reunions). The majority were applauded by the social workers for the efforts they had made in completing or reinforcing life story work, preparing the children for a permanent family and in the manner in which they had altered their own relationship with the children following the placement. However, in around 20 per cent of cases, the behaviour of the previous carers was described as unhelpful or obstructive.

This is well illustrated by one particular case of reunion. Here, prior to moving to the permanent family, three children had been placed with one set of carers while their youngest sister had been placed separately. Contact had been kept up on a regular basis, but the placements had been quite protracted. The foster homes had been very different places, one a noisy and boisterous home, the other warm and quiet in emotional tone. The carer in one case was used to children moving on. She supported the plan for reunion and worked well with the social worker in helping the child to be ready for the move. She made a point of talking to the child after the social worker had visited for the preparation sessions and during quiet moments in the day-to-day routine. The other carers were more ambivalent about the move and in a busy household there was less time, but they were less able to be positive with the children. Conversation about the move was not encouraged, thereby denying the children an opportunity to talk about their anxieties. After the move these differences between the reactions of the two families continued: one carer was able to provide encouragement and support through regular telephone calls, while the other carers' visits and calls were described by the social worker as a "disaster" resulting in upset for everyone involved.

Sometimes these kinds of problems seemed to be due to conflict with social services over plans for the children and sometimes because the children's move was too painful for them to deal with appropriately. Whichever is the case, the finding emphasises the need for sensitive and proactive work with (temporary) foster carers.

Preparatory social work

Social workers were asked to describe the work that had been undertaken with the children to help them understand what had happened to them in the past and why they were moving to a new family. These descriptions were then rated by interviewers to give an overall indication of how much direct preparation each child had received. The accounts showed that the children either had little preparation or that the amount of work was substantial. This overall rating took a variety of factors into account including the age, circumstances and understanding of the child as well as the kind and quantity of work done. For sibling groups, we then

Table 4. 2

The amount of preparatory work by social workers for singletons and siblings groups

	Singly placed (n = 30)	Sibling groups (n = 38)
All children little or no work	46%	24%
Substantial work for some children	–	18%
Substantial work for all children	54%	58%

assessed whether all the children in the group had received a similar amount of work or whether the work tended to be geared to the children as individuals. The proportions of each group are shown in Table 4.2.

Nearly half of the singly placed children were rated as receiving little or no preparatory work. This lack of preparation was less the case for sibling groups but in a quarter of cases no child received an adequate amount of work and substantial preparation was given to some but not all of the children in a further 18 per cent of cases. Differences in the amount of work with siblings were usually associated with birth order, that is, the older siblings tended to have more work done with them. Interestingly, however, this was not directly related to the *age* of the children. Indeed, among sibling groups, both pre-schoolers and those over 10 were less likely to have received substantial preparatory work than those in the middle ranges (χ^2=14.4, df=4, p<0.01). Among singly placed children there were no differences in relation to age. Children in sibling placements who had been physically or sexually abused were more likely than those not so abused to have substantial preparatory work (χ^2= 7.8 and 7.4 df=2, p<0.05 in both cases). These trends were not apparent among singly placed children.

Administrative arrangements for the placement

Fifteen of the 72 placements were planned as long-term fostering rather than adoption. The proportion of foster placements was similar in single and sibling groups. At the time of the first interview, children placed for adoption had been freed in 25 per cent of cases and hearings were in progress for a further 14 per cent, but no moves had been made in 61 per cent of cases. Birth parents were described as being at least reasonably supportive of the placement plans in 61 per cent of cases but in the remaining 34 per cent of cases (28), birth parents were definitely not in agreement with the placement plan. In six of these cases the children had been freed for adoption and four cases were going through this process, but 13 adoptive placements and five foster placements had been made without legal security and with parents in dispute.

Finally, the new families divided into three fairly equal groups with respect to the financial support they were receiving. About one-third of families had been offered no help at all, one-third were given an allowance up to the time the adoption was finalised, and the remaining third had received guarantees of post-adoption allowances. There were no indications that families who took sibling group placements were more likely to receive financial support.

Overview

This chapter has described the backgrounds of the children prior to placement including the characteristics of their birth parents, the quality and stability of their earlier care, the types of maltreatment they had experienced, and the reason for their separation from home. The role of social workers and previous foster carers in establishing and supporting the placements was described.

There were a number of differences both between the individual children and the placement groups on these variables but, anticipating the chapters to come, many of these differences appeared to be unrelated to outcome. This was the case for the administrative arrangements, the level of direct preparatory work, and the way in which the children's previous carers handled the preparation and transition phases. Although there may be occasions when poor performances by adults in any of these activities may cause difficulties or fail to optimise opportunities, these factors did not show any consistent association with outcome.

The analyses have shown that the experiences of the majority of the children, both prior to leaving their birth families and in some cases subsequent to them as well, were far from ideal. Indeed, they were classically the experiences that create a high risk of psychosocial or developmental problems.

Singly and jointly placed children had similar backgrounds with the exception of scapegoating and rejection, which was more common among the single placements. The length of time children spent with birth families, their experiences of maltreatment, and the level of household discord or violence will be a focus of our examination of factors related to individual and placement group outcomes as well as to the children's sibling relationships. Subsequent chapters will examine the extent to which these factors were related to the progress of the placements over the first year and whether there are implications for preparation of families and type of post-placement support.

KEY POINTS
The children's earlier experiences

- With only one or two exceptions, the sample children had been looked after because their parents were unable or unwilling to parent them adequately.
- For the most part, rates of maltreatment were similar for singly placed and jointly placed children, although scapegoating and rejection by birth parents were more common amongst the single placements.
- Sibling groups of two had often experienced similar types of parenting from their birth families; among larger groups differential parenting experience was common.
- Some children had had an alarming number of moves prior to this placement. However, the number of changes *per se* was not a good predictor of outcome because the reason and the character of the move need to be taken into account.
- Although the actions of previous carers were largely positive, in 20 per cent of cases their behaviour during the preparation, introductions and the transition to the new family was regarded as unhelpful or obstructive. This was often because of their own feelings towards the child.
- Half of singly placed children and one-quarter of sibling groups were recorded as receiving very little or no direct work to prepare them for placement.

---

5   Outcomes after a year in placement

The greater part of the rest of this report is concerned with the outcomes for the children one year after the placements began and tries to explain how the variations in these came about. We shall be doing this both by comparing the success of sibling and singleton placements *as a whole* and by looking at the outcomes for the children considered as *individuals*. Switching between these two types of analysis is inevitably complicated. For this reason it is useful at this point to give an overview of how things turned out.

A key question for practice is whether children in sibling placements "do better" than those placed singly, but a little thought makes it clear that this question is not a simple one. How do we compare the outcomes for two or more children placed together with children placed on their own? Is a poor outcome for one out of several children in a sibling group equivalent to a poor outcome for a singly placed child? If the placement of one child in a sibling group breaks down, should the placement as a whole be thought of as a disrupted one or not? Many questions of this kind arise and will be taken up in the more detailed analyses. At this point we simply outline the outcomes for single versus sibling placements and for the children as individuals but, before we do that, we discuss the issue of missing data and look at the few cases that had disrupted by the end of the first year.

Missing data
Four families who took part at the three-month point later withdrew from the study. This reduced the number of children in the outcome analyses from 133 to 125 and the number of placements from 72 to 68. One of the four withdrawals was a single placement and three were sibling groups. The families withdrew mostly because of increasing difficulties in the placements. The accounts we had from social workers suggested that at least three of these withdrawals could be classified as poor outcomes. In addition seven placements had disrupted. These

parents were interviewed but, naturally, the data we were able to collect were not complete. It was clearly important to include these missing and disrupted cases in the analyses of outcome whenever possible. We were able to use information from the disruption interviews with parents and information from social workers on both kinds of missing data in both cases on some occasions. These data were not sufficient for analyses of the outcomes of individual children placed as part of sibling groups but it was possible to include these cases in many analyses of placement outcomes.

Placement disruption

Placement disruption is often used as the only measure of placement outcomes but it is a very rough measure. A number of placements that have not disrupted may nevertheless be in considerable trouble, so disruption tells us little about the success of the placements overall. Even in the longer term, disruption is too crude an indicator of outcome to be used to examine the psychosocial recovery and development of the children. It is much more valuable for practice to be able to explore variations in the *progress* of placements at the one-year point and we deal with this in the rest of this report. Nevertheless, seven of the 72 placements had disrupted by the end of the first year: a rate of 10 per cent. Five of the disruptions were of singly placed children most of whom had siblings elsewhere in the care system: four had been placed alone in child-free homes, while the fifth had joined a family that had one birth child who was three years older. The other two disruptions were both sibling dyads who moved into child-free homes. Both pairs of siblings were over 10 years old, were showing behaviour that the parents found difficult, and got on badly with each other. In both cases they joined parents who found it hard to cope with the demands placed upon them by the children.

Outcome measures

In this chapter we use two kinds of outcome measure. The first is the parents' own assessments of the balance between positive and negative features in their experience of the placement *as a whole* over the year. The second was an interview assessment of the stability of the

69

placements of the children *individually*, based on the parents' accounts of their satisfaction with placement progress and the degree of attachment that was developing between them and the children. The first measure was mostly appropriate for comparing the outcomes of single versus sibling placements and the second for examining outcomes for individual children. We present the overview of outcomes first on the basis of parental evaluations and secondly, on the evaluation of the stability of individual placements. Before using the evaluations to compare single and sibling placements we consider the overall picture from the parents' point of view.

The new parents' evaluation of the placements at a year

It was clear from the new parents' interviews that there was considerable variation in the ease with which children and families had integrated, even though 90 per cent of placements were continuing at the one year point. For some families the placement had progressed extremely smoothly and new parents were reporting a rewarding, if challenging, experience for both themselves and the children. In other families considerable stress and strain were evident. There were difficulties not only with overt behavioural problems but also with the extent to which the parents felt they were able to make a "connection" with the children.

New parents were asked about the positive and negative impacts of the placement on family life. The balance between these impacts was then examined. For 30 of 68 families, the impact was overwhelmingly positive; a further 13 families acknowledged some negative features but were still very pleased with developments. Nine families presented a fairly evenly balanced picture, while for 16 (including the seven disrupted placements) the story was one of difficulties substantially outweighing any pleasures.

In order to compare the outcomes for these small groupings, we took the three predominantly positive evaluations and contrasted these with the predominantly negative ones. For this analysis we had sufficient data to include the four missing cases and the seven disruptions, giving final group numbers of 53 (74 per cent) positively rated placements and 19 (26 per cent) that were less successful.

Early warning signs

Were there any aspects of the placement process that contributed to these placement difficulties? If there were, the associations would be important for practice. We examined two often-cited areas of potential difficulty: "stretching of preferences" and the ease or otherwise of the introduction of the parents and children to each other.

"Stretching of preferences" is a term introduced by Nelson (1985) to describe the way in which prospective adopters or foster carers may be persuaded to take on children who differ from their "ideal". We looked at the disparity between the new parents' reports of the kind of child they had in mind and the child or children eventually placed with them. While differences with regard to gender or the number of children was not associated with problems, parents who had taken children older than they had originally intended were somewhat more likely to report a difficult year, although not significantly so.

Table 5.1

Proportion of positive evaluations according to match with parental preferences

Characteristic	N=	% Positive evaluation	Significance
Gender of child/ren			
Good match	64	75	n.s.
Some difference	7	57	
Major differences	1	100	
Number of child/ren			
Good match	51	77	n.s.
Some difference	11	66	
Major differences	10	70	
Age of child/ren			
Good match	41	82	$\chi^2=4.96$ (2) p=.084
Some difference	23	65	
Major differences	8	50	

The quality of introductions likewise offered some hints of problems to come but the findings were not straightforward. Those that went

71

smoothly and were described as successful did not necessarily lead to an easy placement and some that started with parental reservations worked out well. However, three of the four families who had experienced *serious* reservations during the introductory period reported the placement as predominantly negative. Although these data do not suggest that reservations in the early stages were necessarily associated with poorer outcome, they should nevertheless be taken seriously right from the start.

Grouping the placements for comparative analyses
In this section we compare the outcomes for single and sibling group placements using the parents' evaluations. As mentioned in Chapter 3, only four of the 32 singly placed children had no siblings at all and a further four had siblings who were already adults. The remaining 24 singly placed children were separated from siblings. While it would have been ideal to be able to analyse the data for these groups of singly placed children separately, there were too few children without dependent siblings for this to be feasible. The singly placed children were thus treated as one group. As far as we could see, there were no differences on any of the outcome measures according to the fact of separation from siblings, although there were signs that the whereabouts of other siblings was important for singly placed children.

We also checked whether the outcomes varied for sibling placements according to whether they had any brothers or sisters elsewhere in the care system who might have been placed with them. This was the case for 24 of the 40 sibling groups. Parents' evaluations were positive for 20 of this group compared with 13 of 16 who had no other looked after siblings. There were no differences between these groups (83 per cent *v.* 81 per cent).

With regard to the existence of siblings elsewhere, there were no significant differences between the groups or between the categories within each group. For this reason, all the analyses that follow simply compare children placed singly and those placed together with one or more siblings.

Factors related to outcome for single and sibling group placements

Family characteristics and placement type

Families who took single children (Table 5.2) were more likely to report a difficult year (38 per cent *v.* 18 per cent), a difference that approached statistical significance (exact test p = 0.07). However, there were no differences within or between the placement groups according to whether the single children went into child-free or established families. There were also no differences in the parents' evaluations between the single and sibling placements according to whether the parents had brought up children before, nor indeed whether they had children of their own at home at the time of the placement. There were no differences related to social class or occupational status.

Table 5.2
New parents' evaluation at a year according to placement configuration

	n=	*Positive evaluation*	*Negative evaluation*
Singly placed with child-free family	19	58%	42%
Singly placed with established family	13	69%	31%
Joint placement with child-free family	36	83%	17%
Joint placement with established family	4	75%	25%

Children's characteristics and experiences in relation to family outcome
Earlier experiences
Group comparisons of the impact of the children's background experiences was not feasible because of the diversity in the experiences of individual children within sibling groups. For example, it was not uncommon for the older children to have experienced sexual abuse, emotional abuse and neglect, while the youngest had escaped all but the neglect. Additionally, there were some cases where one child in a group had been rejected or another had been favoured. These individual experiences cannot be combined into a summary variable that characterises the group as a whole.

Age and gender

Fewer girls than boys were placed singly but when they were, perhaps surprisingly, the placements of girls were less likely to be positively evaluated by parents (45 per cent for girls compared with 71 per cent for boys), a substantial but not a significant difference. The gender mix of the children in sibling groups showed no association with the way in which new parents described the placements nor was the age of the eldest child significantly related to parental evaluation for either singletons or sibling groups.

Current psychosocial problems

The new parents' evaluations for both singly placed and jointly placed children were significantly associated with persisting problems in the children's interactions both with the parents themselves and with their own or their new siblings. Forty per cent of the sibling group placements where some or all of the children had difficulty with child–parent interaction were negatively evaluated, compared with three per cent of placements where there were no such problems. Among singly placed children these proportions were 70 per cent versus 19 per cent respectively. Difficulties in the relationships between the children themselves were also significantly associated with parents' negative evaluations. Even though the scenario for single children joining new siblings was substantially different from that for children moving to new families with their own siblings, poorer parental evaluations were likely in the presence of sibling interaction difficulties in both cases. We should also mention that difficulties with the new siblings were reported in two of the four cases in which sibling groups joined established families. One of these was evaluated positively and one negatively; both of the cases with no sibling problems were categorised as good outcome. These data are presented with statistical tests in Table A.2 of Appendix I.

Interestingly, there was a difference between the single and sibling placements in the degree to which the children's levels of emotional and behavioural problems influenced the parents' judgements. Surprisingly, the problems seemed to have had an influence for single but not for sibling placements. This finding is counter-intuitive. It may be expected that emotional and behavioural problems might be more strongly related to poor evaluations of placements for sibling groups simply because of the sheer quantity of such problems, but this was not the case. Reasons for these differences are discussed in more detail in Chapter 6.

Summary of outcome by placement type

Overall, viewed from the perspective of the parents' experiences over the course of the first year, around three-quarters of placements were described as progressing well. The first year had been substantially more difficult for the remaining 19 families and indeed in seven of these cases the placement had already ended. Families who had single children placed with them were somewhat more likely to evaluate the placement negatively. There were no differences according to whether the new parents already had children of their own and there were no differences between children who were separated from brothers or sisters and those who were not. There were some indications that parents who took children who were older than anticipated experienced more difficulties. There were also suggestions that parents who had early and *significant* reservations about whether they and the matched children were right for each other had a more difficult year. Factors found to be consistently associated with the parents' evaluations were the children's interaction patterns, both with their new parents and with brothers and sisters. However, these characteristics are more properly individual properties of the children and should be more closely examined in that context.

Variations in placement stability for individual children

We now move on from the discussion of the outcomes for single compared with sibling placements to present some data on the outcomes for individual children. In later chapters, these two ways of looking at outcomes will be put together when we consider placement type as one of the variables influencing individual outcomes. Here we introduce the concept of placement stability and look at how the children were progressing.

Assessing placement stability

The assessment of *placement stability* combined maternal and paternal responses to questions about their attachment to each child and their degree of satisfaction with the child as a member of the family: that is, two scores from the mother and two from the father. The ratings for each parent on each of these two dimensions were scored as: no attachment/ satisfaction (score 0); some problems (score 1); satisfactory attachment/ satisfaction (score 2). The parents' four scores were then summed to produce a score ranging from 0, meaning very little indication of attachment or satisfaction from *either* parent, to 8 indicating that *both* parents were reporting adequate feelings of attachment to and satisfaction with the child. For most analyses this score was dichotomised with a score of 4–8, meaning that there were at least reasonable reports of attachment and satisfaction from both parents or good reports from one parent. A score of 3 or less suggested that both parents were experiencing reservations or more serious problems.

The placements of the majority of the children (100 of 125) were rated as stable on this measure at the end of the first year. We then examined which features of the children's experiences and current circumstances were related to stability and instability. Children whose placement had disrupted were included in the unstable group.

Factors associated with placement stability for individual children

Type of placement

Table 5.3 gives the first key comparison: the levels of stability for children in sibling and singleton placements and variations in stability according to whether the children were placed in child-free or established families.

One-third of singly placed children were in less stable placements compared with 16 per cent of children who were placed with their brothers or sisters, a large difference that just fell short of the 5 per cent level of significance (exact test p = 0.069). Among singly placed children there were no differences according to whether the new family was child-free or had birth children at home.

Table 5.3
Placement stability for individual children according to placement configuration

	n=	More stable	Less stable
Singly placed with child-free family	19	63%	37%
Singly placed with established family	12	75%	25%
Joint placement with child-free family	85	88%	12%
Joint placement with established family	9	44%	56%

For sibling groups there was a substantial difference between family type, with five of the nine siblings joining established families showing poor stability (exact test p = 0.005). This difference is highly significant but it should be noted that the number of placements with established families was very low. This small but problematic group of sibling placements into established families was also "responsible" for reducing the singleton versus sibling placement comparison to marginal significance. It should be noted that the difference between singletons and siblings placed in child-free families was highly significant, to the advantage of the sibling placements (exact test p = 0.014).

Associations with children's characteristics and experiences
The associations between the stability of placements and the children's characteristics and experiences are given in Table 5.4. But, before moving on to examine these associations in more detail, it is worth emphasising the areas of difference between single and joint placements. These are indicated by the solid diamond shapes in Table 5.4. Among this sample of children, singly placed children were more likely than those jointly placed to be male (p = .068) and to have experienced rejection (p = .066). They were also more likely than siblings to show problems with child–parent interaction at both the three-month and the twelve-month interviews, although the differences were more marked at the early point (p = .001 and .063 at 3 and 12 months respectively).

Table 5.4
Factors associated with placement stability for individual children (n = 125)

	Singly placed (31)			Jointly placed (94)		
Factor	*N*	*% stable (21)*	*p*	*N*	*% stable (79)*	*P*
Age at placement						
under 5	0	–		17	100%	
5–10	26	69%	–	58	83%	•
Over 10	5	60%		19	74%	
Gender ◆						
Boys	21	76%	–	44	86%	–
Girls	10	50%		50	82%	
Sexual abuse						
No	21	71%	–	60	90%	*
Yes	10	60%		34	74%	
Physical abuse						
No	20	60%	–	54	91%	*
Yes	11	82%		40	75%	
Emotional abuse						
No	7	100%	–	19	84%	–
Yes	24	58%		75	84%	
Rejection ◆						
No	21	81%	*	82	82%	–
Yes	10	40%		12	100%	
Neglect						
No	7	71%	–	14	79%	–
Yes	24	67%		80	85%	
High behaviour score 3/12						
No	15	13%	–	60	83%	–
Yes	14	43%		34	85%	
High behaviour score 12/12						
No	15	13%	–	60	83%	–
Yes	14	43%		34	85%	

Factor	N	Singly placed (31) % stable (21)	p	N	Jointly placed (94) % stable (79)	P
Poor child–parent interaction 3/12 ◆						
No	23	81%	**	82	85%	
Yes	8	40%		7	80%	–
Poor child–parent interaction 12/12 ◆						
No	21	86%	**	80	87%	*
Yes	10	30%		14	64%	
Problem with siblings 3/12						
No	8	75%	–	55	91%	*
Yes	4	75%		38	74%	
Problem with siblings 12/12						
No	10	90%	*	61	92%	**
Yes	2	0%		32	69%	

* Denotes group differences are significant at p<0.05 **p<0.01.
◆ Denotes marked or significant differences between singly and jointly placed children, see text for details. Group differences tested using χ^2 or Fisher's exact test for categorical data.

Age and gender

There was no difference between boys and girls but the children's age when they joined their new families was an important factor in the outcome for those placed with siblings (there were no young children in the singly placed group). It is clear that the placement of younger siblings was the most successful and that the risk of a poorer outcome rose with age (Exact Cochrane-Armitage test for trends p = 0.01). There was no age trend for the children who were singly placed.

Age structure

The analysis of the influence of age structure is complicated and a full statistical treatment would require many more children than were available to our analyses. Nevertheless, we tried to see whether there appeared to be any benefits in being placed with siblings within broad age groups.

We have already seen that sibling placements involving children over 10 only were particularly problematic. However, as is clear from Table 5.5, there were no significant differences in placement stability for individual children according to the presence or absence of younger siblings.

Table 5.5
Outcome according to age group and the age group of siblings

	Number of children	% stable	
Child over 10			
Sibling/s also 10+	13	69	n.s.
Sibling/s 5–9	6	83	
1 or more pre-school sib	–		
Child 5–9			
Sibling/s 10+	7	86	n.s.
Siblings also 5–9	26	73	
1 or more pre-school sib	25	92	
Pre-school child	17	100	

Numbers reduced due to missing 12 month data

The children's prior experiences

Neither the number of previous placement moves nor the social workers' reports of potential difficulties because of existing attachments were related to stability for either singly or jointly placed children. Children who had experienced sexual abuse were less likely to be in stable placements. This was true for both singletons and sibling groups, although the differences were only significant for the latter group. The curious reversed position, where the experience of physical abuse was associated with higher placement stability for singletons, was not statistically significant. This pattern was not repeated for sibling groups. The great majority of the children had experienced neglect. For this reason alone we were unable to detect an association between neglect and stability. It should be remembered that testing for bivariate associations only holds a number of perils. First, of course the majority of these children had been maltreated in one way or another so the lack of one kind of abuse did not imply a lack of abuse overall. Secondly, the lack of associations with a particular form of abuse does not mean that this experience has no ill effects. It simply means that it did not stand out as a predictor in this maltreated sample.

Our earlier study (Quinton, Rushton, Dance and Mayes, 1998) highlighted the strong association between poor outcomes and the experience of being singled out and rejected by birth parents. This finding was replicated here for the singleton placements but not for those placed with siblings. The implications of this difference are discussed later. At this point we should note that rejection was especially associated with poorer placement stability for boys. Thus five of 15 rejected boys had a poor stability while this was true for only one of seven girls.

As is clear from Table 5.4, experiences of rejection among children placed with siblings were relatively unusual; nevertheless, it is the case that social workers described some children as having experienced a much more negative emotional environment within their family of origin than was true for their brothers and sisters. However, the removal of rejected children along with their siblings was likely to have been precipitated by other adversities and not by the rejection itself. For these children, therefore, the separation might not have been experienced as a personal rejection in the way that it might for children placed on their own.

The children's behaviour
The impact of the children's psychosocial difficulties are presented in more detail in Chapter 6. We draw on these data at this point in order to explore the relative importance of these factors when considering outcomes for individual children. The overall level of emotional and behavioural problems shown by the children at either three months or a year were not significantly related to placement stability, although there were some interesting differences between the two groups. However, in common with the findings for outcomes at the family level, specific aspects of the children's behaviour did relate to placement stability. Thus the quality of child–parent interaction was especially important for singly placed children and predicted outcome from the early stages of placement. Children placed with siblings were less likely to be described as

having such difficulties. When they were, the problems were not significantly associated with outcome. However, poorer placement stability was strongly associated with problems in sibling relationships.

Variation in stability within placements

In this section we briefly consider the variation in individual outcomes *within* placements, that is, we look at the extent to which the outcomes for jointly placed children vary. The first task was to explore what the extent of this variation was: that is, whether the pattern of individual outcomes tended to be true for all children in a family or whether there were families in which the placement was stable for some children but less so for others. In practice, in the great majority of new families, the placements of *all* of the children were classified as stable. However, there was a small proportion of sibling group placements where the outcomes were mixed. In these four cases (11 per cent of sibling group placements), one child was assessed as having a poor outcome while others in the same placement were considered to be stable.

Nathan is a case in point. He was placed with his two younger siblings in a child-free family. All three children showed some behavioural problems but nothing alarming: some lying, some over-activity and tantrums and the occasional streak of defiance. On the whole, all three children related well to their new parents. Nathan, however, tended to bully his sisters whenever the opportunity arose. He would also try to hurt them physically, sometimes by throwing objects at them, sometimes by stabbing them with a pencil or something similar. Importantly, he appeared to show no remorse when his behaviour led to tears on the part of the younger children. Although the new parents recognised that the younger ones tended to play up their tearful reactions, they still found Nathan's cruel streak hard to deal with on an emotional level, finding it more difficult to see him as settling with them and more difficult to feel close to him.

Three of the four families evaluated their *overall* experience positively, despite their difficulties with the one child. This may be important if, in the longer term, the satisfactory progress of some siblings leads to a more secure placement for children whose early progress is poor.

No further analysis was possible for this very small group. A case-by-case examination of the group revealed no clear pattern of influences except that all four cases involved placements of three or more children; the unsettled children varied in their place in the age structure of the placement but three of the four were girls.

Overview

This chapter has reviewed patterns of outcome a year after placement. Of course, one year in placement is a short time. Some placements that were in difficulty at this point may go on to become more secure. On the other hand, our earlier study (Quinton *et al*, 1998) showed that many of the early signs of difficulty of placements do have longer term predictive consequences. Furthermore, greater understanding about *which* children or *which* placements may be vulnerable has implications for planning, preparation as well as support.

Seven of the 72 placements had disrupted by the end of the first year: a rate of 10 per cent.

The parents' evaluation of the impact of the placement, whether singleton or sibling group, on the family as a whole showed that 26 per cent of placements (16 of 72) were classified as poor outcome at one year. There was no evidence that sibling group placements were less stable or more problematic than the placement of single children. Indeed, where there were differences, these were generally to the benefit of sibling placements.

Eighty per cent of the 125 individual children for whom information was available were considered to be in stable placements at the end of the first year. The associations between outcome and particular experiences in the children's histories were found to differ depending on whether children were placed alone or with their brothers and sisters. Thus sexual and physical abuse was associated with poorer outcome for jointly placed children, while emotional abuse and rejection by birth parents were particularly important for singletons.

The relationship between general behavioural difficulties and outcome were inconsistent. This will be discussed in more detail in subsequent chapters. However, the parental evaluations of the placements and the measure of stability were both related to problems in the children's relationships with parents and with siblings. The chapters that follow will develop a fuller picture of these outcomes, exploring the factors associated with them in single and sibling group placements. Most importantly, we will move, as far as we are able, towards some conclusions about the advisability of single and sibling placements and to understand what underlies the differences between the two whenever these appear.

KEY POINTS
Outcomes after a year in placement

- Seven of 72 placements disrupted in the first year (10 per cent).
- The impact of the placement was positive for 74 per cent of new families. The first year had been less successful for 26 per cent.
- Families who took single children were more likely to report a difficult year.
- Among singly placed children, scapegoating and rejection by birth parents were associated with poorer placement outcome, especially for boys. However, when placed together with siblings, the relationship between rejection and poor outcome did not hold.
- For both groups, poor placement outcome was most closely associated with difficulties in the children's interaction with either the new parents or with their siblings.

---

6 The children's behaviour and relationships

In the previous chapter, we showed how difficulties in the children's behaviour and relationships were associated with the parents' evaluation of the progress of the placements overall and how such problems were related to our assessments of the stability of the placement for each child. In this chapter, we consider the children's emotional and behavioural problems in more detail, with a particular focus on their impact on the children's relationships with other family members. These analyses focus predominantly on problems at the individual level but we also consider the patterns of relationships within groups of children.

We begin by looking at the new parents' overall views on the children's behaviour at a year, in order to give a feel for the sorts of difficulties that had been persistent and troublesome. This section is followed by one that compares the kind and level of problems shown by the placed children compared with children in the general population who were being raised in their birth families. This comparison is made using an established questionnaire filled in by the parents, which indicates the level and kind of problems the children were showing (The Goodman Strengths & Difficulties Questionnaire(1994)). Finally, we look in more detail at the new parents' accounts of the children's problems using a standard interview measure of emotional and behavioural difficulties – the Parental Account of Children's Symptoms (PACS – see Appendix). We supplemented this interview with additional questions covering problems that are more common in maltreated children than in other groups, for example, questions on sexualised or parentified behaviour. These questionnaire and interview measures were described in Chapter 2.

Parents' broad descriptions of difficulties

In the one-year interview, parents were asked how the children were getting on in seven areas: openness and affection, conduct, emotional difficulties, schoolwork, relationships with siblings, peer relationships and play. Table 6.1 shows the proportion of children showing notable problems in each of these areas and compares singly placed children with those placed with siblings. There were no significant differences between the two groups but singly placed children were somewhat more

Table 6.1

The frequency of moderate to major behavioural and interaction difficulties at one year for children placed with and without siblings (n = 117 for all variables except sibling interaction. Missing data due to disruptions and case withdrawal)

	Singly placed %	Placed with a sibling %	all %
Openness/affection	26	12	15
Conduct	41	28	31
Emotional	33	30	31
Academic	37	38	37
Sibling interaction	31	31	31
Peer interaction	11	26	22
Play	18	21	21

prone to exhibit difficulties in openness or affection and to show more conduct problems.

Overall, roughly one-third of the children showed conduct and emotional difficulties, problems with siblings, and difficulties at school. About one-fifth had ongoing problems with peer relationships and play.

Almost all of the new parents (97 per cent) reported that there had been some level of change over the course of the year in at least one of these areas. For the majority (77 per cent), all the changes that they had noted were in a positive direction, even though aspects of the children's behaviour might still have been difficult. Twelve per cent of parents had noticed both improvement and deterioration in their children. For only eight per cent of children were all changes reported to be in an undesirable direction.

Overall, just under 40 per cent of placed children were classified as not having any major problems at the one-year point, while 28 per cent had significant difficulties in three or more of these areas. The proportions were similar for singly and jointly placed children and there were no differences according to whether there were birth children in the new family. Boys showed slightly more difficulties than girls and pre-school children slightly fewer than those over five, but these differences were not significant.

The children's difficulties compared with children in the general population

The majority of new parents completed Goodman's (1994) Strengths and Difficulties Questionnaire (SDQ) at the time of the one-year interview. The same data were collected from 100 families in the general population. Details of the comparison sample and of the SDQ are given

Figure 6.1
Mean scores on SDQ problem sub-scales for sample and control children

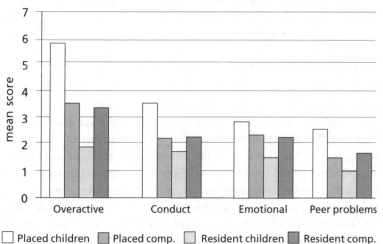

The mean emotional scores for placed children and their comparisons were substantially but not significantly different (F = 3.186 (1,281) p = 0.056) scores on all other sub-scales differed significantly (F ranged from 21–46 (1,281) p<0.001)

in Chapter 2. Questionnaires were missing for 22 placed children. In most cases this was due to placements having disrupted or to the new parents declining the second interview. Both of these circumstances are likely to have been associated with high levels of difficulty. For this reason, the figures may underestimate the true level of problems among the placed children and this should be taken into account when interpreting the data. It seems likely that the differences between the placed and comparison groups would have been greater if the missing data had been available. It is therefore possible, but not certain, that marginally significant differences would have become significant.

The SDQ produces an *overall score* ranging from 0–40 and *sub-scales* that indicate the level of functioning in five separate domains: pro-social behaviour; conduct; emotional difficulties; over-activity and problems with peers. A score of 17 or greater on the overall scale has been shown to indicate a level of difficulty that is outside the normal range. We were able to compare both the placed children and the new parents' birth children with the comparison group. The mean scores on the four difficulty scales for placed children and birth children along with the two control groups are illustrated in Figure 6.1. (Separate comparison groups were used for placed and birth children because of the disparity in age between the two.)

The placed children differed significantly from the comparison group on the overall score and on all sub-scores apart from emotional problems, which was just short of the 5 per cent level of significance. The pro-social scale is not included in the chart, but placed children scored significantly lower than the general population group (mean scores 6.7 as against 7.9). Looking at the differences in terms of the cut-off, 46 per cent of placed singletons and 38 per cent of jointly placed children scored 17 or more on the problem scales as opposed to 13.5 per cent of the comparison group (χ^2=26.8, df = 2, p<.001). The comparison children followed the usual pattern in the general population as far as gender differences were concerned, with girls scoring significantly lower than boys on over-activity, conduct problems and total score (F = 3.8–4.4 (1,176) p< = 0.05). Gender differences amongst the placed children followed a common pattern in high psychosocial risk samples with *no* significant differences apart from a higher score on emotional problems

(F = 5.6 (1,103) p<.05). Resident birth children did not differ significantly from their comparison group on any of the measures.

It is important to note that there were *no* differences between single and sibling placements. This is the first piece of evidence to hint that the differences in outcome in favour of sibling placements was not simply a consequence of children placed as siblings having generally lower levels of problems. On the other hand, these questionnaire scales were taken at the one-year point. Looking at *predictions* of difficulties according to the level of problems early on in the placement must wait until we consider the interview accounts.

These findings confirm that late placed children, both boys and girls, are at risk for a wide range of problems. The differences between them and the comparison groups were particularly large for over-active and restless behaviour, a finding consistent with our previous study. On the other hand, it should be noted that the scores covered a wide range (0–34) and that, even given the adversities in their earlier experiences, over half (54 per cent) scored under the cut-off for problems overall. Figure 6.2 illustrates how the range of scores was wide for both placed and control children, but the difference in distribution is evident.

Figure 6.2

The frequency of total problem scores for sample and comparison children

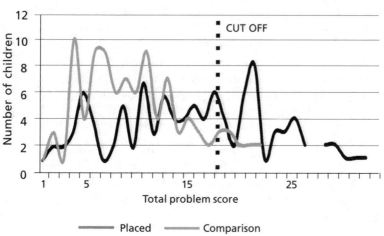

The children's problems as recorded by the PACS interview

The PACS interview (Parental Account of Children's Symptoms) takes parents systematically through a series of questions focused on the behaviour of their children. The range of the 35 problems covered is shown in Table A.3 (see Appendix). The presence and severity of emotional and behavioural problems are rated by the interviewer on the basis of detailed parental accounts of how the problems show themselves. A problem is rated only if it has a clear negative impact on the family or the child's life. This usually means that the problem is both quite severe and happens frequently. However, some less frequently occurring behaviours nevertheless have an enduring impact and these are also rated as problems.

The PACS can be used to provide a count of the number of difficulties and also a score for problems in three specific areas: emotional difficulties like anxiety, worrying and fears; conduct problems like defiance, lying and fighting; and problems with overactivity, restlessness and poor concentration. In addition to the standard PACS items covering these problems, we included 16 items (at the bottom of Table A.3) which other research, including our own, has highlighted for children in substitute care. These difficulties are rare in the general population, but are likely to be more common in late placed children. For the most part they reflect problems in relationships with adults and might now come under the general heading of "attachment difficulties" but include other problems such as sexualised behaviour, rocking and self-harm. It was important to document the frequency of these problems even though some are not generally included in inventories of psychiatric difficulties. They may presage more persistent difficulties or may be transitory. In either case, knowledge of them should help in the preparation and support of placements.

Table A.3 in the Appendix details the frequency with which these individual psychosocial difficulties were reported for children of different ages at three months and a year. Here we provide a summary of the findings. The interested reader can examine the table in the Appendix for the full details.

The most common problems concerned activity, attention, lying and defiance. Difficulties with overactivitity and poor concentration were evident for roughly one-third to two-fifths of children in all age groups and were relatively stable throughout the year. Lying, tempers, defiance to parents and irritability were, if anything even more common, especially for the older children, with two-fifths to one-half or more of children aged five or over showing such problems. Defiance towards other adults was not uncommon among the older age group, neither was aggression towards peers, although this latter problem declined markedly over the year. Eating problems occurred towards the end of the year for about one-fifth of younger and older children, but not for the middle age range. The most common of the emotional problems was the presence of fears or phobias that affected around 40 per cent of children under the age of 11. Within the older group, manifest worrying was more often a feature and showed a rise over the year with nearly 30 per cent worrying to an extent that affected their lives.

Among the problems we added to the PACS, rocking or significant self-harming occurred only rarely but the decision to include the other behaviours proved very revealing. Two-fifths of children were described as showing an unusual response to pain either by being grossly melo-dramatic about minor mishaps or by being overly stoical. Some children showed a strange mixture of making a tremendous fuss about minor bumps and scratches but hiding any sign of hurt after more serious incidents. Parents reported episodes of significant regressive behaviour or a more generalised immaturity for around a quarter of the children. Between 10 and 20 per cent of children showed a tendency either to pester their parents, above and beyond what would normally be expected from youngsters of their age or to have a pattern of repeatedly asking the same questions. These tendencies were not overly common but parents reported them as very draining and often difficult to handle. Around one-third of children were described as being resistant to tackling new challenges either by a hostile refusal to try, usually by dismissing them as something "stupid", or an insistence that they would not be able to do it.

For the most part the children showed an ability to differentiate their parents from other adults in providing comfort or setting boundaries.

The children generally accepted affection from their new parents and were spontaneously affectionate towards them, although lack of spontaneity was more common among the oldest children. These older children were also less likely than the younger ones to show appropriate comfort-seeking behaviour.

However, a proportion of parents were unsure about the genuineness of the affection they received from the children, especially from the older ones. An over-friendly approach towards strangers was evident for nearly half the children at the start of placement, particularly for the younger two age groups, although this diminished during the year for many of them.

We used the data from the additional items to create a scale of difficulties in interaction with adults. The items included were: lack of age-appropriate comfort-seeking behaviour; an unusual response to pain or hurt; a lack of spontaneous affection; resistance to physical affection; displays of affection seen as non-genuine or "phoney"; a lack of differentiation of parents from other adults and over-friendliness towards strangers. This scale will be used alongside the standard PACS sub-scales in the analyses that follow.

The final item we asked about was sexualised behaviour, which was not common among younger children but was a feature for around a quarter of those over five at the beginning of placement and showed some increase over the year. The behaviours that warranted a rating on this item included masturbation, either to an unusual extent or in unusual circumstances, and sexually provocative physical interaction with adults or other children.

The children's behaviour in placement

At three months into placement, the average overall PACS score for the whole sample was 5.6 (range: 0–21, s.d. 4.3), indicating that the children were showing an average of five or six significant problems. There was no significant change in the overall score by the end of the year (mean 6.0, range 0–23; s.d. 4.8), nor were there any differences at either point between children in single or joint placements, or between the broad age groups. At the three-month point, boys' scores were significantly higher than girls' scores (F = 7.0 (1,131) p<0.01), but this difference had disappeared by 12 months, mainly due to a substantial but non-significant rise in the average score for girls.

We found when examining the sub-scores that, apart from a significant rise in the level of conduct difficulties shown by girls placed with siblings, the mean scores stayed relatively stable regardless of the children's gender, age group or whether they were placed jointly or singly.

Behaviour and its relationship with placement stability
Overall behaviour scores were discussed briefly in Chapter 5 when we considered outcomes. Here we look in more detail at the various areas of difficulty and whether these showed any association with placement stability.

There were no significant differences in any of the four sub-scores according to age group or gender at either time point. The average scores of singly and jointly placed children on most of the sub-scales were similar, but there were substantial differences between these two groups in their mean scores on the interaction difficulties sub-scale. There were no differences according to whether the children were placed with child-free or established families. Abusive experiences in the past showed no relationship with the conduct, emotional or overactivity difficulties for either children placed with siblings or those placed alone. However, significant differences were found for the interaction scores. These associations are considered later.

Exploring the mean scores for singly and jointly placed children, according to whether or not their placements were considered stable at a year revealed very little difference in any of the three-month scores for either group, with the exception of the adult interaction scores for singly placed children. The latter score was predictive of lower stability at a year from the three-month interview.

At the one-year point, the children in less stable single placements had significantly higher overall scores, conduct scores and interaction scores than more stable singletons. Singly placed children whose place-ments were in difficulty showed a worsening of behaviour on these scales while those whose placements were seen as stable showed some improvement. This pattern was not repeated among children placed with siblings. For jointly placed children, *none* of the three-month measures was predictive of less stable placements and a lack of stability was not associated with a rise in emotional or behavioural problems. The only measure associated with placement difficulties was the rating of interaction with adults at 12 months. (These data are presented in detail in Table A.4 of Appendix I.)

These data are very interesting. Among children placed with siblings, most types of behaviour difficulties, at either point, were not related to the stability of their placements. In contrast, singly placed children in stable placements tended to show a reduction in their mean level of difficulties, while those in less stable placements showed an increase over the course of the year. We shall explore the reasons for these differences in more detail in subsequent chapters. However, it is important to point out here that the data clearly show that the differences in levels of stability for children in single and sibling placements are not to be explained simply by the levels of difficulty of the children going into the two different kinds of placement. In the next section we explore one possibility: whether the parents' toleration of difficulties was greater in sibling placements, especially where at least some of the children were settling in well.

Behaviour of sibling groups
In order to examine the patterns in sibling groups, it was necessary to simplify the ratings. To do this we turned the overall score and each of the four sub-scores at each point in time into binary scores indicating a high or low level of difficulty and then examined those cases where there were persistent or worsening difficulties over the course of the year. For each type of difficulty, a score in excess of 1.5 standard deviations from the mean was taken as indicative of a high level of problems.

Around half of the new parents reported that all of their children were relatively problem free, one-third said that at least one child showed more difficult behaviour and around 20 per cent of families were comprised entirely of problematic children. This pattern was similar regardless of the number of children in the sibling group, although there were no cases of placements of four children in which all were classified as difficult (much to the relief of the new parents, we would suspect).

Table 6.2
Proportions of children with sub-types of behavioural problems in singleton and sibling group placements

	Singles n = 29	Sibling groups n = 37
No enduring conduct problems	76%	54%
Some children with conduct problems	–	35%
All children with conduct problems	24%	11%
No enduring emotional problems	76%	62%
Some children with emotional problems	–	30%
All children with emotional problems	24%	8%
No enduring over-activity	69%	46%
Some children overactive throughout	–	46%
All children overactive throughout	31%	8%
None with high interaction problems	68%	73%
Some with high interaction problems	–	22%
All with high interaction problems	32%	5%

The sub-scales (Table 6.2) showed that families who took sibling groups were somewhat more likely than those who took single children to have at least one child with difficulties, but in only a minority of cases were all the siblings classified as having a high level of problems. Of course, the action of taking more than one child will increase the probability of the placement containing at least one child with difficulties.

There was no evidence that parents' assessment of difficulties was greater in groups with a higher proportion of boys and no suggestion that age gaps or the ages of the children were related to the proportion of difficult children in each group. Even when there were problems, these did not appear related to whether new parents viewed the placement overall in a positive way. Thus the majority of sibling placements were classified as stable even when all the siblings were considered difficult.

As we have indicated, there is a greater chance of having at least one member of a sibling group showing increased levels of behaviour problems. One explanation for better outcomes for sibling groups might be that the level of tolerance on the part of parents who take sibling groups is higher. This might be because the presence of other siblings reduces the amount of focused attention on any one of the children. This could in turn affect parental behaviour since the child's misdeeds may have less of an impact, that is, recovery of the parent's good humour and acceptance of the child may be swifter if there is another distraction. It might also be the case that another child in the group may provide sufficient parental reward despite the presence of more difficult children.

Examining children's problems in adult interactions

The associations between problems in interactions with adults and the progress of both singleton and sibling placements are a striking feature of the data presented so far. This section looks at this group of difficulties in more detail and examines its overlap with earlier experiences and other emotional and behavioural problems.

Overlap with other problems

Before assuming that interaction difficulties were especially important in their own right, it was necessary to check the overlap between these difficulties and other kinds of problems. Perhaps interaction difficulties signalled that the children had a wide range of problems. This was in fact the case. Children classified as having persisting or worsening interaction problems showed significantly more overall psychosocial difficulties, conduct problems and emotional problems, although they were not more likely to be overactive or restless. Thus the presence of interaction problems did identify a group of children with substantial difficulties. This overlap needs to be taken into account when examining the implications of interaction difficulties.

Associated experiences

As we pointed out earlier, although abusive experiences in the past showed no relationship with the conduct, emotional or overactivity difficulties, they were related to interaction scores.

A comparison of singleton and sibling placements on adult interaction problems according to earlier experiences of maltreatment is given in

Table A.5 (see Appendix). Looking first at different sorts of maltreatment separately we found emotional abuse, rejection by birth parents, and sexual abuse to be the experiences that were significantly associated with child–parent interaction difficulties. However, the extent of association varied according to whether children were singly or jointly placed. For example, while seven of ten rejected singletons were showing a high level of these problems, none of the twelve rejected children who were placed with siblings were. Of course, many children had experienced more than one type of abuse, therefore we computed a combination variable that indicated the extent to which each child had experienced maltreatment of this sort. The mean scores on the interaction difficulties scale according to type of emotional abuse are presented in Table A.5 (see Appendix). For both groups a combination of sexual and emotional abuse carried a higher risk of child–parent interaction problems. Among singly placed children the strongest and most consistent relationship between earlier experiences and interaction problems was undoubtedly with rejection by birth parents. However, for jointly placed children, at the twelve-month point the associations with rejection went significantly in the opposite direction to what might have been expected.

What does one make of this complex picture? The first possibility is that these variations are due to the vagaries in the identification of different kinds of maltreatment, that is, they are an artefact of the unreliability of the data on background experiences. However, there is no obvious way in which this ought to affect singleton and sibling data differently. The alternative is that rejection, although clearly described for the sibling as well as the singleton placements, carried a different meaning for the rejected members of sibling groups, perhaps because the act of placement was not experienced as a personal rejection. It might even have been experienced as a relief. On the other hand, attachment theory would have led to the prediction that the children in both singleton and sibling groups would have had problematic internal working models of relationships with adults and would be likely to have developed interaction styles to protect themselves from hurt and confusion. We had no measures of the children's internal models, but the behavioural outcomes suggested a significantly different set of representations for the children in sibling placements, if working models are the mediating mechanism in this instance.

It is also possible, more prosaically, that the parental perceptions of rejected children who were placed with siblings may have been influenced by their relationships with the other children in the group.

Before proceeding further, it may be helpful to provide some examples of the circumstances we are referring to. The cases are not "typical" because each child and family are unique; nevertheless, they are illustrative of the sorts of difficulties experienced.

Laura was one of five children; all had been looked after for short periods but she was the only one of the family that was not wanted back. Her time with her birth mother had been fraught, particularly after a younger sibling died (of natural causes) when her mother made it clear that she would have preferred that it was Laura who had died. She spent a considerable time being reasonably settled with a foster family who had a number of other children around the home, both their own and other foster children. The foster family lived relatively near Laura's home town. At the age of 10, after a considerable amount of life story work, Laura moved some distance, to an adoptive family who had no children of their own. According to the prospective adopters, on paper it was a reasonably good match, that is, there were no negative feelings towards the child but neither was there anything to indicate that these parents and this child were positively right for each other. Speaking with hindsight (at the three-month interview) the adopters felt from the start that Laura did not want a new mother; indeed, she told them that she already had a mother and did not need another. She was much more accepting of her new father. These feelings were evident during the introductions but the adults hoped that relationships would improve. However, over the course of the next six months or so, Laura's behaviour towards the adoptive mother proceeded to get more and more challenging, including lying, stealing and physical aggression. Her moods could swing in an instant and she would fly off the handle at the smallest thing. Even a comment such as 'that looks nice' from the mother would provoke an antagonistic outburst leading eventually to a temper tantrum. Laura would not engage in any mutual way with her adoptive mother, refused food prepared by her, would not tolerate physical contact with her, and even resisted being in the same room with her. The mother's experience in this case was set against that of the father who would be greeted from work enthusiastically. Laura enjoyed sitting with him and would talk to him in a normal manner and she would even on occasion confide in him. In this case, there were disagreements between the professionals involved about the level of specialist help required and the timing of it. In the event, a referral to Child Mental Health Services was made but, despite the urgency, the waiting list was long and the placement ended a few weeks before the first appointment was due.

In contrast, the placements of rejected children within sibling groups seemed to proceed relatively well. There was only one case in which the rejected child had not developed quite such a good relationship with his new mother as he had with his new father, but even here it was judged by the mother to be very similar on both sides. In all of the other cases, the relationships with rejected children were described as mutual and as good with both parents. On the odd occasion that there were variations in the quality of relationships with different children, the parents' relationship with the rejected sibling tended to be better than that with non-rejected children. This does not mean that the rejected children were necessarily the easiest of children. Some of the new parents talked about difficulties, eventually overcome, in reaching them emotionally. One mother talked about how tackling the difficulties successfully enabled a special closeness to grow with the rejected child. This child was the middle child of a group of three who had been severely scapegoated in the birth family. At one point there had been discussion about returning her two siblings to their birth mother and her remaining in care alone. Her siblings, particularly the older one, perpetuated the scapegoating into the new placement. The rejected child did have a difficult time in the first year. She was emotionally insecure, over-friendly to strangers, and unable to show feelings of fear or anxiety in an appropriate way. The adopters perceived that she was more comfortable with the father than the mother. But throughout she had been accepting of both new parents and had no difficulty in giving or accepting affection. Part way through the year, she went through a very difficult stage with violent temper tantrums. The family was fortunate in securing family therapy at the time, which helped them to formulate ways of helping this child. By the second interview, although the child continued to be very vulnerable, the adopters were able to recognise when things were worrying her and, with their encouragement, she had learned to be able to talk about her fears. For the most part this defused the violent behaviour. The parents felt she had attached to both of them and they both felt close to her. They found it less easy to be close to the older child who, as well as bullying the younger ones and blaming the rejected child for their being in care, continued to identify strongly with the birth mother.

There were of course two major differences between the first and second case. Not only was the second child placed with her siblings, the latter family was also successful in securing timely therapeutic assistance. Undoubtedly, this had a positive impact on the placement and the child's emotional development. However, a positive relationship had already developed between the adopters and this child.

Another less common circumstance involved cases where more than one child had been rejected by the birth family and placed together, while other children remained at home. This tended to be associated with the birth mother embarking on a new relationship and a new family as happened in the case of two young girls. Their birth mother had rejected them as toddlers and they then spent some time with their birth father, but were then ejected from the home when he and their stepmother had children of their own. Permanence plans were made relatively quickly, but a first set of introductions failed. The elder child's comment at that point was telling: 'She didn't like us. You'll get it right next time, won't you?' The two children were very different characters and each had their own problems with regard to their behaviours and their social interaction; however, they related to their new parents well and rapidly settled together into their new family.

There clearly seemed to be a difference between the experience of children who had been scapegoated or rejected and placed alone and those who had similar experiences yet moved with their brothers and sisters.

There remains one situation we have not illustrated: that is, those cases in which rejected children were placed singly but parents reported a positive year. Three of these four cases were extremely demanding of the new carers. As usual, the mothers bore the brunt of problems, at least partially because they did most of the day-to-day caring. In these three cases the mothers displayed outstanding patience, understanding and tolerance of defiant, aggressive and uncontrolled behaviour. Also common among them was the ability of the children to give and receive affection. One case might illustrate this point.

Nick was five when he was placed following a series of short-term placements and repeated attempts at rehabilitation. At placement his new parents described him as a shy little boy, but angry with his birth family and confused about why he was in care and his brother was not. He was also an intelligent child who often asked questions about his past that the adults did not have answers for. Alongside this he had periods of two to three days at a time of continual tantrum like behaviour with extended screaming and aggressive outbursts. Despite these problems, the new parents, reflecting on the year, said it had been a tough one and the placement could well have disrupted except that Nick was immensely affectionate, even when in a bad mood, which resulted in them feeling very attached to him. Consequently, they had never entertained the idea of ending the placement; they had, however, asked for and received substantial support from the family social worker.

There remain questions about the psychological impact of experiences and the behaviour or attributional style of new parents that cannot be directly answered by the data available, but there are other avenues we can explore. Firstly, it is possible that much more work had been done with children in sibling groups who had been scapegoated or rejected. Secondly, the differential meaning of rejection according to the type of placement might be reflected in measures that tap the level of the child's confusion or anger – feelings that might influence future relationships.

Direct work

Was there any evidence that the work done with sibling groups and singly placed children differed? We looked at the records of the experiences of individual children and the interviewer's rating of the amount of direct work the child/ren had received and found that the work was quite randomly distributed. More or less half the children in each group received either little or no work while the other half were rated as having had moderate or considerable work. This held true regardless of the abuse experiences of the child or group. Our earlier study concluded that the amount of direct work was more related to the experience and confidence of the practitioner than the level of need as indicated by the child's experiences or difficulties (Quinton *et al*, 1998). It is very likely that this factor accounts for the variation in this instance also.

Therapy

The picture with regards to therapy was different. There were no differences in the proportions of singly placed children or sibling groups referred for therapy, but those placed alone were somewhat more frequently offered help that continued beyond the assessment stage: 9 of 15 referrals compared to 6 of 18 referrals of children in sibling groups. In both groups, sexually abused children were more likely to have received therapy ($\chi^2 = 8.3$ (2) p<.02 for singles; $\chi^2 = 8$ (2) p<0.05 for sibling groups), although the abusive experience was rarely the reason given for the referral. Rather, the majority of children in both groups were referred for help with behaviour problems. Strikingly, in this sample, 30 per cent of singletons and 15 per cent of children in sibling groups were being helped with bereavement. In neither group was there any indication that a rejecting experience may have been the prompt to refer for therapy.

Interestingly, 35 per cent of children classified as having interaction difficulties had received some form of therapy compared with only 12 per cent of children without these problems ($\chi^2=5.9$, (1) p = 0.051). There was no indication, however, that the children who had received therapy were scoring substantially differently on the overall behaviour scales. This suggests that the rating of interaction difficulties was genuinely tapping an important aspect of the children's behaviour that was giving professionals cause for concern.

Siblings elsewhere

Was rejection worse for singletons and jointly placed children who had siblings living elsewhere? Ten singleton placements involved rejected children and there were 11 sibling groups with one or more rejected children. Nine of the former and seven of the latter had "siblings elsewhere". In both groups, children who had been rejected were equally likely to have siblings at home so the whereabouts of siblings was not the answer to the differential effects of rejection. However, for all the sibling groups, the brothers or sisters who were at home were considerably younger than the placed children. Indeed, in five of the six cases, these siblings were less than a year old at the time of placement and had certainly been born subsequent to the placed children leaving home. Among rejected singletons this was not the case. The "other siblings" were much closer in age to them and were, indeed, equally likely to be older as younger.

These data do point towards the association between rejection and placement carrying different meanings for children placed singly and those placed with sibling groups. For the singletons, their individual rejection went along with continuing acceptance of the other children in the family, whereas children rejected within placed sibling groups have a degree of shared experience with their brothers and sisters in that they left the birth family together, their siblings at home usually being children they have never lived with and probably do not even know.

Overview

This chapter has explored the emotional and behavioural problems of the children, as reported by their new parents, as well as a new measure of problems in relationships with adults. Differences according to age and gender were not striking, although some problems showed predictable associations with age. Comparisons were also made between single and sibling group placements in the level and pattern of problems for individual children, and differences between them were related to the children's previous experiences. Consistently with other studies, the overall levels of emotional and behaviour problems were high, especially as regards overactive, restless and inattentive behaviour. Problems in conduct and high levels of worrying and anxiety were also common. However, the most striking feature was the frequency with which the children showed problems in relationships with their new parents and other adults.

Few background or placement factors had a dramatic or consistent impact on the level of emotional or behavioural difficulties shown by the children during the first year in placement nor was the level of those difficulties necessarily associated with placement stability by the end of the year. However, children who had marked difficulties with child – parent interaction were less likely to be in stable placements and this association was much stronger among singly placed children. Difficulties in interactions with adults were related to the children's experiences of emotional and sexual abuse and of scapegoating and rejection. Few children in either group who had not suffered emotional abuse or rejection had difficulties in relationships with adults. However, the pattern of associations was different for the rejected children in singleton and sibling placements. Most notably, the rejected children in sibling groups did not seem to be at risk of showing poor patterns of relationships with their new parents and other adults. This may point to a fundamental difference in the meaning of "rejection" for the two groups. The analysis also raised questions about parents' attributional style and their response to the children's rejecting behaviours.

KEY POINTS
The children's behaviour and relationships

- From the parents' accounts, about one-third of children showed conduct and emotional difficulties, problems with siblings, and difficulties at school. About one-fifth had ongoing problems with peer relationships and play.
- There were no significant differences between the two groups but singly placed children were somewhat more prone to exhibit difficulties in openness or affection and to show more conduct problems.
- Late placed children, both boys and girls, were at risk for a wide range of problems. The differences between them and the comparison group were particularly marked for overactive and restless behaviour.
- The systematic assessment showed that the most common problems concerned overactivity, poor attention and defiance.

- Two-fifths were described as showing an unusual response to pain, either by being grossly melodramatic about minor mishaps or by being over-stoical. Not uncommon was a mixture of the two.
- Parents reported regressive behaviour and immaturity for a quarter of the children.
- Lack of genuine affection was evident among some older children and over-friendliness to strangers for some of the younger ones.
- There was no significant change in overall problem scores by the end of the year, nor were there any differences at either point between children in single or joint placements.
- The differences in levels of stability for children in single and sibling placements are not to be explained simply by the level of difficulty of the children going into the two different kinds of placement.
- Rejection by birth parents was associated with later problems in interaction with adults for children placed singly but not for siblings placed together. We suggest that, for the singletons, their individual rejection went along with continuing acceptance of other children in their family, whereas children rejected within placed sibling groups have a degree of shared experience with their brothers and sisters in that they left their birth family together.

7 The character of sibling relationships

We saw in Chapter 5 that the new parents' perceptions of the placement and our assessment of placement stability at a year were strongly influenced by difficulties in sibling relationships. In this and the next two chapters we go into these relationships in much more detail. We were interested firstly to explore whether the ways in which placed siblings behaved towards each other were different from the relationships they had with the birth children of their new parents. Next, we wanted to know whether difficulties in relationships were related to the children's early experiences and whether they were confined to these relationships or whether they were part of more general emotional or behavioural problems. Finally, we wanted to know whether adoptive sibling relationships differed from those of children who grew up in their own families. This last comparison used the data from the general population sample. These issues are dealt with in this chapter. Chapters 8 and 9 give the details of the types of relationship difficulties faced by new parents as well as details of the interventions by social workers and others that were designed to help with these problems.

In this chapter we examine sibling relationships using three different types of information from the parents' accounts at three and 12 months into the placements. The first analyses involve the parents' descriptions of the children *as a group*. Next, the questionnaire data are used to look at the relationships between each *dyad* within a group. Finally, we consider *each child's behaviour* towards his or her siblings using the detailed information from the interviews. Some information from the comparison sample was available for the first and second of these analyses.

The relationships between siblings as a group

As a reminder, there were 72 new families in the study. Thirty-six of these involved sibling groups who joined child-free families. A further 13 singly placed children and four sibling groups joined families with resident birth children. Nineteen children were placed on their own in child-free homes and are therefore not appropriate to this chapter because they had no siblings in their households. In these analyses, therefore, the majority of placements that involved sibling relationships were either of children placed with their own brothers or sisters in child-free families or children placed on their own in families with resident birth children ("established families"). Clearly the tasks for the children and the parents are very different in these two scenarios. The four sibling groups who joined established families comprised too small a group to analyse separately. We make some observations on these placements later. Otherwise, these cases were excluded from the analysis of group interactions since their experiences may have been substantially different from those of the other two groups.

Parents' concerns about sibling interaction
The parents' descriptions of the relationships between the children as a group were given first and before we asked in detail about the relationships between individual children and their siblings. Parents were encouraged to air their concerns about any aspect of the sibling interaction, without hints from interviewers about what they should talk about or what the interviewers thought was important. Figure 7.1 shows the *main* worries of the parents at three months and again at the end of the year. We focused here on the main worries but this is not to suggest that there were no anxieties about other aspects of the children's interaction.

Problems were significantly more commonly identified among placed sibling groups than between singly placed children and their new siblings. The accounts were dominated by concerns over *disputes* between the placed siblings. These rows and squabbles will surface several times in the course of this chapter in one guise or another.

Two other main types of problems were *rivalry* between the children, defined as competition for parental attention, and *parentification*. The latter was usually a problem for one child, usually the eldest in a group and often a girl. The "parentified" child adopted a quasi-parental role, undertaking both nurturing and discipline responsibilities with the younger children to a greater extent than is true of most older children. This behaviour was a common source of concern to parents in the early

107

Figure 7.1

Parent concerns about sibling relationships at 3 and 12 months after placement

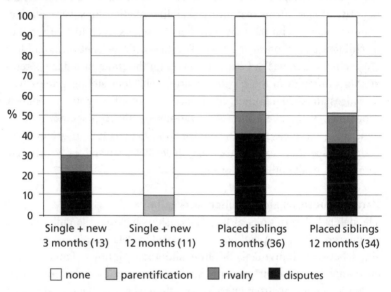

months. They often found it difficult to work out how best to help the child relinquish the role without losing self-esteem and establish their own role as parent. However, as illustrated in Figure 7.1, this problem was relatively short-lived in most cases indicating that, despite the difficulties, most of the parents found ways of doing this successfully.

A notable feature is the absence of problems with their new siblings for the group placed on their own in established families. Although they are only a small group, very few parents indicated any major concerns over the relationships between the children. However, these data do conceal some difficulties. In particular, the two cases for whom data were missing at one year had experienced significant problems between the children and, in one case at least, these had been instrumental in the placement ending. In one case these disputes were evident at three months and are represented in the chart.

Siblings' feelings for each other

At the three-month point, the relationships among placed sibling groups were seen as predominantly positive in 45 per cent of cases, but at the other extreme, parents saw no positive features at all in 22 per cent of the placements. The relationships in this latter group showed marked improvement over the year and parents reported at least some positive feelings between the children in six of the eight cases that had been described very negatively at three months. There were no cases in which parents found cause for concern increasing over the year.

As far as the children singly placed into new sibling groups were concerned, over half of the parents felt that positive feelings were developing between the children by the three-month point (52 per cent) and in only one case were these feelings thought to be entirely negative. By the end of the first year things looked even better, with predominantly positive relationships described for 82 per cent of the placements and the remaining 18 per cent showing positive feelings at times. The one case in this group with very poor sibling relationships from the start of the placement disrupted before the end of the year.

We asked about other features of the sibling group interaction, such as the extent to which they shared memories about the past and were inclusive or exclusive of other children. These questions did not, however, reveal any real patterns and there was a good deal of inconsistency over time. Of course, the new parents could only be aware of the detail of the interaction between the children if it happened openly in front of them. It is likely that some such discussion may have taken place outside the home or behind closed doors. There were, however, some examples of placed children using each others' memories to confirm their own impressions. Differences were also apparent in children's interpretation of experiences which sometimes caused substantial problems. For example, one child had completely re-written her past, exonerating her birth mother entirely, while her sibling felt the painful memories of the mother's inadequate parenting keenly. Another child who was trying hard to integrate at school under her cover story was very distressed when her sibling, at the same school, felt the need to "tell it as it was" in unedited fashion to anyone who would listen. The extent to which children needed to talk to each other or took advantage of the opportunity varied from case to case and indeed within placements both between children and over time. Some youngsters raised issues at the meal table which led to open discussion. In other cases the mention of the past by one child could be too much for others to deal with. Undoubtedly, there will be circumstances in which children will get much from the opportunity to share their memories, but it is important that those involved with placements are aware that it can cause difficulties at times.

Differences between the sample and comparison sibling groups
The parents in the general population comparison group gave us some information about sibling relationships within their families. There were some differences in the sibling group structure of the placed and comparison groups that might affect the analyses and we tried to reduce these as much as possible. Potentially the most important of these was that the placed sibling groups tended to be closer in age. For this reason, the comparison group was restricted to families where the ages and age spread of the siblings were reasonably similar to that of the placed children and where full group interaction data were available. This procedure resulted in 39 comparison families for the sibling groups placed in child-free families and 18 comparison families for children placed singly into new sibling groups. The data on this matching procedure are given in the Appendix (Table A.6). There were no significant differences in the structure of the sibling groups in these two comparisons. We were able to compare the degree of joint activity, rivalry, and frequency and severity of disputes between siblings in the two different types of placement and their comparisons. In order to keep these analyses as clear as possible, we discuss these findings for the two placement configurations separately.

Interaction among siblings placed together in child-free homes
Table 7.1 gives the data on the sibling group placements. The columns show the patterns of interaction at three and 12 months and compare these with the relationships in the control sample.

The level of joint activity showed very similar patterns across the sample and comparison groups. These similarities contrasted starkly with

Table 7.1
Group interaction for placed siblings and their comparison group

	Placed sibling groups		Control	
	3 months $n = 36$	12 months $n = 34$	Once $n = 39$	
Joint activities				
No activities as a group	11%	18%	5%	a) n.s.
Some	39%	30%	29%	b) n.s.
Frequent	50%	53%	66%	
Rivalry				
None or occasional only	36%	47%	82%	a) $\chi^2= 17$, p< 0.005
Regular for at least				b) $\chi^2=10$, p<0.005
Some children	64%	53%	18%	
Frequency of disputes				
Infrequent < 4 a week	28%	41%	78%	a) $\chi^2=19$, p< 0.005
Frequent 4 + a week	72%	59%	78%	b) $\chi^2=10$, p< 0.005
Severity of disputes				
No fighting	58%	68%	92%	a) $\chi^2=11$, p<0.005
Includes fighting	42%	32%	8%	b) $\chi^2=6.6$, p< 0.05

a) significance at 3/12   b) significance at 12/12.

the other features of the children's relationships: rivalry and the frequency and severity of conflict were markedly elevated among placed sibling groups.

Joint activities
Most of the siblings in both groups interacted on a fairly regular basis with only a small minority avoiding joint activities altogether. These patterns were true regardless of the number of children or the gender mix of the sibling group, but older siblings and those who had larger age gaps tended to do less together. These latter differences were more marked for placed siblings but the patterns were similar in the control group, suggesting that the extent of joint activities is likely to be

111

influenced by both the ages of the individual children and the spread of ages within the group. It was not at all surprising to find that younger children spent more time with their siblings since they were likely to have more restricted access to peers and out-of-home activities. Equally, children close in age were likely to be at closer developmental stages and thus more able to share similar interests.

Rivalry

Rivalry was specifically defined as competition between the children for parental attention. This is a feature that is quite common among sibling groups, indeed fewer than one-quarter of control parents said that it never occurred in their families. However, we were concentrating on evidence of marked rivalry such as one child "muscling in" on another child's story time, or repeatedly distracting a parent from attending to a sibling, or frequent complaints about a brother or sister always getting more or getting something first. As with most of our measures, parent reports changed for some groups over the course of the year. One-fifth of new parents described no significant competition at either interview and early difficulties in this regard settled over time for a similar proportion. However, one-quarter thought these problems were developing and 35 per cent found their children to be competitive throughout.

Rivalry as a group feature did not appear to be related to the structure of the sibling groups. Neither the placed siblings nor their comparison group showed *within group* differences in rivalry according to the number of children in the family, the gender mix of the children, the ages or the age spread of siblings. However, there were some interesting differences *between the groups*. Placed sibling groups headed by boys showed more rivalry than their comparisons, but not significantly so; however, placed groups headed by girls showed markedly more rivalry than their counterparts ($\chi^2 = 12.9$ (1) p<0.001). In the comparison group there was a tendency for rivalry to decrease with larger age gaps between the children, but this was not reflected among placed children. Similarly, within the comparison group, rivalry was uncommon where the eldest child was over 10, while it was reported by 78 per cent of sample parents with children of this age. The picture then was one of much more competition among the placed children which, in some cases, was sustained over a longer age range than was true for siblings growing up in their birth families.

The high level of rivalry among the placed children was not a major worry for many parents. It is possible that this reflects the belief that rivalry is a normal part of everyday life when there is more than one child in the home. Certainly, the interviewers became used to hearing the phrase "no more than any other brothers/sisters" in response to their questions on this subject. However, it is also likely that where both rivalry and disputes were present, the degree of conflict was uppermost in terms of causing anxiety for parents and the role of rivalry in causing conflict less clear.

Disputes

Disputes were both more frequent and more severe than in the comparison families. Only 22 per cent of comparison group parents reported significant disputes at least every other day, compared to 72 per cent of placed sibling groups. The control groups' disputes were usually verbal arguments and in only 8 per cent was serious fighting reported, whereas 42 per cent of placed sibling groups resorted to physical fighting on a regular basis. Neither the frequency nor the severity of disputes between placed siblings showed very much sign of improvement over the year and 32 per cent continued to use physical means to settle arguments.

The pattern of conflict was not related to the number of children in a sibling group in either comparison or sample families, but there was a gender effect. For both groups more frequent and more severe disputes were reported for male-only groups while all female groups had frequent conflicts in a minority of cases only. However, there was an interesting difference between the sample and comparisons in terms of mixed gender sibling groups. Within the sample these groups were similar to all boy groups in their patterns of conflict, while among comparison cases, mixed gender groups were more akin to female only groups. Regardless of whether headed by boys or girls, mixed groups of placed children showed significantly more conflict than their comparison groups. From the group perspective, there were no differences in the character of conflict for either group according to the age of the eldest child, nor indeed according to the age gaps between children. As is clear from

Table 7.1, although there was some reduction in the levels of conflict over the first year of placement, frequent and serious disputes remained a characteristic feature of a substantial proportion of sibling group placements.

Interaction between singly placed children and their new siblings
Table 7.2 provides the information on the sibling groups consisting of one placed child and the birth children of the new family. As pointed out elsewhere, the numbers of placements of this type were very low; nevertheless, it is worthwhile describing the parents' perceptions of the interaction between the children.

The most striking feature of Table 7.2, in comparison with Table 7.1,

Table 7.2

Group interaction between singly placed children and new siblings and their comparison group

	Single + new siblings		Control	Significance
	3 months	*12 months*	*Once*	
	n = 13	*n = 11*	*n = 18*	
Joint activities				
No activities as a group	23%	18%	11%	a) n.s.
Some	54%	64%	39%	b) n.s.
Frequent	23%	18%	50%	
Rivalry				
None or occasional only	54%	42%	89%	a) $\chi^2= 4.8$, p< 0.05
Regular for at least				b) $\chi^2=7.6$, p<0.05
Some children	46%	58%	11%	
Frequency of disputes				
Infrequent < 4 a week	54%	64%	78%	a) n.s.
Frequent 4 + a week	46%	36%	22%	b) n.s.
Severity of disputes				
No fighting	86%	100%	92%	a) n.s.
Includes fighting	15%	–	8%	b) n.s.

a) significance at 3/12   b) significance at 12/12.

is the lack of significant difference between sample and comparison groups. New sibling groups were rather less likely to be described as joining in activities together, but the difference was not significant, and the majority did so at times. Disputes were slightly more frequent for sample children but tended to be verbal only. The only significant differences involved rivalry between the children or young people. This was reported significantly more frequently by the new parents than was true for the comparison group and this persisted, indeed worsened, over the course of the year. The group was too small to allow for any serious examination of whether gender, age or number of children had any bearing on the extent of conflict or activities together, but no obvious patterns emerged for either group.

That rivalry should be a feature of new sibling placements is not particularly surprising: the placed child is likely to feel a need to find a role and reassurance of position when joining children who have an established history in the family. Equally, the previously resident children are likely to require confirmation of their continued importance. Rivalry might also be exacerbated because of a need for parents to purchase material goods and to spend substantial amounts of time in helping the placed child with academic work.

Overview of group relationships

The above examination of group relationships has shown that new parents perceived and described the relationships between their children quite differently from parents in the general population. Relationships between brothers and sisters who were placed together were particularly likely to be described as conflictual, although this tended to occur in groups who also played together. Rivalry was more frequent between both placed siblings and new sibling groups than was true for the control group.

It should be noted that the patterns of relationships amongst the two comparison groups were very similar despite differences in their age structures. Further, the differences in relationships between the two types of placement and their comparisons were similar, apart from a lower level of joint activities in the new sibling groups of singly placed children and few severe disputes within these new sibling groups compared with those placed as siblings. The contribution of the placed and birth children to these patterns is considered below.

Dyadic relationships

The preceding section explored relationships within sibling groups as a whole. These groups varied in size, gender mix and age characteristics. While there were indications that these factors had some impact on the level of difficulty in some contexts, they by no means explained all of the variance. Although high levels of conflict and rivalry were identified within families, these difficulties were not necessarily focused upon all the children within a family. We next look in more detail at relationships between pairs of children. In order to set the context for this analysis it is necessary to clarify the pattern of these dyadic relationships within the families (Table 7.3).

There were 135 pairs of siblings in the sample: 85 of two placed children, 37 comprising one placed child and one new sibling, and 13 where both children in the dyad were birth children of the new family. Naturally, the number of possible dyads increases markedly as the number of children in the family rises. It will be clear from this that gathering data on each pair of relationships was time-consuming particularly for the larger families.

Table 7.3
The number of dyadic relationships in the sample

Number of children in a family	Number of dyads resulting	Number of cases in sample	Total dyads in sample
2 children	1	26	26
3 children	3	19	57
4 children	6	7	42
5 children	10	1	10
		53	135
1 child	no dyads	19	None

The complexity of these data means that they have been through a number of processing phases in order to make them presentable. At each point we have tried to present our rationale for collapsing the information. As we mentioned earlier in this chapter, we had two sources of information about dyadic sibling relationships: the Furman Sibling Relationships questionnaire completed by the parents and the interview ratings based on the parents' accounts. We begin with the analyses based on the questionnaire data. This allowed us to examine three dimensions of a sibling relationship: warmth and closeness, conflict, and relative status and power. We also use the questionnaire data from the comparison sample. These were completed by parents for one dyad within their family.

Treatment of missing data

There were a number of missing questionnaires for the sample dyads, particularly at the 12-month point. In order to simplify the presentation, the analyses include only those pairs for whom data were available at both time points. These data were available for a total of 92 sample dyads (80 per cent of all possible dyads) and 100 comparison dyads. The sample was divided into three distinct types of dyad: a) those comprising two placed siblings; b) those including one placed child and one resident birth child (new sibling); and c) information concerning two resident birth children (new siblings). Dyads for whom data were missing at 12 months were found to have shown *fewer* problems of conflict and unbalanced power relationships at three months. There was no difference between the two groups in terms of the warmth shown by the children to each other.

We can surmise that those parents whose children's sibling relationships appeared unremarkable to them, saw less reason to complete the questionnaires, possibly because they felt that there was little that their experience over the year could add to what they had said before. This assumption is backed anecdotally by the interviewers, who sometimes encountered reluctance among those families where sibling relationships were unproblematic. It does, of course, mean that conflict difficulties may be somewhat over-represented.

Our second check, which examined the consistency of these reports over time, showed a remarkably high degree of agreement on all factors between the three-month and 12-month reports for all three of the sample groups. Comparison data were only collected once, although they were used in relation to both sets of sample data.

Sibling relationships in different types of dyad

The sub-scale scores for warmth, conflict and relative status and power were examined using Analysis of Variance to reveal any differences between the means of each of three sample groups and the comparison group.

Relative status and power

This was a measure of whether the relationship was characterised by equality or whether one sibling dominated the other. There was only one difference between the groups on this measure, with the birth children in families with singly placed children being more dominant. This is unsurprising given that the birth children were often much older than the placed child, were secure in their family, and frequently took on an overt caring or nurturing role with the incoming child.

Warmth and conflict

The more interesting findings related to the patterns of reported warmth and conflict. The mean scores on each dimension for each group and at each time point are given in Table 7.4. There were no significant differences between the comparison group and those sample dyads composed of two resident birth children. These relationships were rated as reasonably balanced with mean warmth scores being higher than conflict scores. If there were any differences between the birth children and their comparison group, the relationships of the birth children were characterised by even more warmth and less conflict than the comparison group. In contrast, dyads made up of a birth and a placed child showed lower levels of warmth than was true for the two groups of birth children. Interestingly, dyads involving placed and birth children also showed *lower* levels of conflict than pairs of birth children. This contrasted with the pairs of placed children, where conflict scores were higher than all other pairings, although not all of these differences reached statistical significance. We checked whether differences in the age and gender structure of these groups made a difference to the mean scores but they did not.

Table 7.4

Mean sub-scale scores at 3 and 12 months according to type of dyad

Type of dyad	N=	Warmth 3/12	Conflict 3/12	Warmth 12/12	Conflict 12/12
2 placed children	62	8.6*	9.0	8.8*	9.1*
1 placed and 1 resident child	28	8.0*	6.0*	8.4*	5.8*
2 resident children	9	10.3	7.0	10.0	6.8
2 comparison children	101	9.9	8.1	9.9	8.1

F=9.2 (3,196) F=9.4 (3,196) F=6.3 (3,196) F=15.4 (3,196)
p<0.001   p<0.001   p<0.001   p<0.001

* The mean score for this group differs significantly from the relevant comparison group score, determined using Tukeys post hoc procedure.

The picture emerging from these data is then a complex one. Siblings placed together showed higher levels of conflict and lower levels of warmth than the comparison children, especially by the end of the year. Relationships between resident and incoming children showed relatively little conflict but were also lower in warmth. This was perhaps unsurprising at the initial interview but it should be noted that this pattern was the same at the end of the year. Relationships between two resident birth children tended to be, if anything, more warm and less conflicted than was true for the general population group.

Taking account of sibling group sizes

At this point one issue needs to be dealt with. The analyses presented above compared the averages for all dyads for which data were available within each group. As mentioned at the beginning of the chapter, sometimes as many as four siblings were placed together, resulting in six dyads, and one family reported on 10 dyadic relationships. In these larger sibling groups, information concerning any one child would have been included several times. If one child had extremely poor or extremely good relationships with all siblings this would clearly have an impact on averaged information.

In practice, in these larger families, good relationships existed between *all* of the children in only one-third of cases and poor relationships between *all* the children occurred in only one case. However, it was important to exclude the possibility that bias was being introduced in the analyses because of the inclusion of all dyads within a placement. In order to check for this, two comparisons were conducted. The first comparison involved a randomly selected pair of placed children and the second the "best dyadic relationship" in any one family as evidenced by the level of the warmth/closeness.

The first of these two procedures resulted in a slight decrease in the average warmth score for placed siblings at both points in time and an increase in the mean conflict scores. The differences between the placed dyads and comparison group dyads were significant over both conflict and warmth at both points in time under the random selection method. When we selected the "best dyadic relationship" among placed siblings, we found that warmth scores increased for the placed group and the probability of the observed difference occurring by chance increased to .087 and .070 at three and 12 months respectively. However, average conflict scores were still significantly higher at both points in time (F = 5.292 at 3 months and 4.23 at 12 months, d.f. =1,129, p<.05 in both cases). These procedures confirm that differences between placed sibling pairs and other dyads were not being distorted by the very poor functioning of individual children. We have been unable to find more sophisticated statistical procedures for dealing with this problem.

Relationships according to age and gender characteristics of siblings

Scores on the various dimensions of the sibling relationship questionnaire are known to vary according to the ages of the children, the age gap between them, and the gender of each child (Furman and Buhrmester, 1985). However, the existing data concern children who have not had the extreme experiences that characterise the early childhoods of our placed children. It is therefore necessary to look at the age and gender patterns separately for the comparison and the placed children. This was possible for placed sibling groups but there were too few children in the other two groups (placed plus birth children and two birth children) to make these analyses possible.

Comparison children

There was a tendency within the comparison group for warmth to be higher in dyads of the same gender but gender composition showed no relationship with the degree of conflict reported. Similarly, the age of the eldest child in the dyad did not affect conflict and warmth scores, but the *difference in age gaps* proved to be important. There was a clear tendency for warmth to be greater among those who were closer in age. Conflict scores were lower for those very close and very distant in age compared with dyads with age gaps of between 2 and 5 years. These findings are similar to those reported by Furman and Buhrmester (1985) with the exception of lower levels of conflict between very closely spaced siblings.

Placed children

Dyads composed of two placed children showed different patterns. For them there was no sign of the expected differences in warmth according to gender. At the three-month point, pairs of boys were showing higher levels of conflict than mixed gender or girl pairs but these differences had disappeared by 12 months because conflict among the boys decreased and increased for the other gender combinations. The effects of age differences on warmth were similar to the group: those closer in age showed more warmth. However, there were no differences in the level of conflict according to age.

Patterns of dyadic relationships

So far, these analyses of the sibling questionnaire data have looked at average scores on the three main dimensions that the questionnaire measures: warmth, conflict and dominance. However, it is also necessary to put these dimensions together and to try to group the relationships into some simple and meaningful categories. In order to do this, we used the comparison sample as the basis for defining high and low scores on the dimensions that differentiated the samples – warmth and conflict –

and then used these definitions to look at differences between the samples in more detail. These scores took the points that marked the upper and lower 25 per cent comparison pairs on these dimensions. Three types of relationship were defined:

- distant relationships characterised by low warmth and low conflict;
- conflicted relationships characterised by low warmth and high conflict;
- warm or moderately warm relationships not dominated by conflict.

The data on these three groups are given in Table 7.5.

Table 7.5
Predominant description of relationships for placed, resident and comparison children according to questionnaire responses

Type of dyad	N =	Distant		Conflicted		Mostly warm	
		3/12	12/12	3/12	12/12	3/12	12/12
2 placed children	62	14%	13%	37%	38%	49%	48%
1 placed and							
1 resident child	28	47%	46%	29%	18%	25%	36%
2 resident children	9	11%	11%	–	–	89%	89%
2 comparison children	101	6%		18%		76%	

Group differences at 3/12 χ^2 = 45.3 (6) p<0.001; at 12/12 χ^2 = 41.9 (6) p<0.001

It is clear from the table that the relationships of birth children, in both the study and the comparison samples, were predominantly warm, although about one-fifth of them were conflicted. Placed siblings were much more likely to be conflicted and less likely to be predominantly warm but only a few of them were distant. This is strikingly different from the relationships between placed and birth children, which were most usually distant. These relationships showed some increase in warmth and some decrease in conflict over the year but there was no change in the proportions of distant relationships.

Overview of the character of sibling relationships among placed children

So far we have shown very large differences between sample and comparison children in the quality of their sibling relationships. This was true both on the parents' overall account of the children seen as a group and on their ratings of the relationships between pairs of children. It was true both for children placed with their own siblings and for those who had new siblings as a result of joining established families. However, the way in which each of these groups differed from the comparison children was not the same. Placed sibling groups showed high levels of conflict and relatively low levels of warmth.

What predicts poor sibling relationships?

Of course, it is hardly surprising to find that the sibling relationships of children placed permanently in alternative families are more problematic than those of children raised in less problematic birth families. On the other hand, the patterns of relationships showed considerable variation and it is important to see whether there were any predictors of these differences and whether these sibling problems are specific to these relationships or part of a more general pattern of psycho-social disturbance.

In order to take this further, it was necessary to draw on our third source of data – the parents' detailed accounts of the children's sibling relationships and social functioning. Using these data we constructed an index that described each child's style of sibling interaction. In the next section of this chapter we examine this index in relation to the data already presented and then utilise it to explore associations between emotional or behavioural problems, past experiences, parent–child relationships, and sibling interaction.

The children's propensity for positive sibling relationships

From the interview data concerning sibling relationships, we were able to look more closely at the ways in which the children's relationships with each other might overlap with settling into their new families and the degree of stability of their placements.

We were able to categorise each child according to the level of warmth or caring and the degree of antagonism or confrontation shown towards siblings. Within this we also took account of whether a child's difficulties tended to be with just some siblings or all of them. Children were rated positively whenever there was any evidence of them showing care and concern for a sibling, even if they may have other siblings with whom they clashed. Having categorised each child in this way, we were then able to make a judgement on whether sibling relationships were a problem for just one or some of the children in a placement or whether all of the children had problems.

Concentrating on the 40 placed sibling groups, we found that at three months 46 per cent of parents indicated no major problems in the way their children related to each other. They quarrelled of course, but no more than would be expected for their ages and the initiator of disputes and squabbles could be any one of them. Of the remainder, half reported that some of their children had problems in their approach to the others and the other half (27 per cent of the total in each case) reported that all of their children had difficulties in relating to each other. Membership of these groups was remarkably consistent over the year, with only nine of 37 families, for whom data were available, describing changes in the children's relationships that were sufficient to warrant a different categorisation, four in a positive direction and five negative. At three months, there was a tendency for problems with some children in a sibling group to be more common in larger families (three or more children) than was true for twosomes ($\chi^2 = 5.9$, df $= 2$, p $= .053$). However, this difference had disappeared by 12 months.

As might be expected from what has gone before, these groupings were found to be associated with the parents' evaluations of the placement ($\chi^2 = 5.1$ and 8.4, df $= 2$, p $= .080$ and $.015$ for sibling interaction problems at three months and one year respectively). However, it was of interest to look a little more closely at whether there were particular characteristics that were associated with poor outcome for individual children. At three months into placement, over half of the 101 jointly placed children for whom data were available (55 per cent) were described as interacting fairly well with their brothers and sisters. They showed a reasonable degree of caring about their siblings and were not excessively confrontational. Twenty-three children were thought to show more conflict than normal for their age but this occurred within the context of caring about their siblings. A third group, accounting for 15 children (15 per cent), also showed high levels of antagonism towards their brothers and sisters, but in this case it occurred without any warmth or caring towards the others. For the final group, comprising just eight children, parents described a rather distant approach, characterised by a lack of caring or interest in their siblings but with little confrontation. This group was quite small for analysis so groupings were reduced to those without conflict problems, conflict in the context of a caring approach and conflict without much evidence of caring for others.

There was a small amount of change in these characteristics over the year, with six children developing a more appropriate approach towards their siblings and 11 children showing more difficulties in this regard. At both time-points, the placements of children who interacted positively with their siblings were much more likely to be classified as stable at the end of the year, although this was more noticeable when looking at the classification at a year ($\chi^2 = 8.4$, df$= 2$, p$= .015$, $\chi^2 = 19$, df$= 2$, p$= .000$; three and 12 months respectively). The placements of the group that showed a high conflict level in combination with a relative lack of care

Table 7.6

The interaction between problems with sibling relationships and high levels of psychosocial problems

	3 months		12 months	
	N=	Proportion with a high behaviour score	N=	Proportion with a high behaviour score
Normal conflict & caring	56	21%	51	16%
High conflict, normal caring	20	55%	16	69%
High conflict, lack of caring	14	57%	17	77%

towards siblings were most likely to be classified as unstable at a year.

Table 7.6 illustrates how, at both three and 12 months, the children who had an antagonistic approach towards their siblings, regardless of whether or not they showed any caring, tended to also show high levels of behavioural problems at both points in time. It seems likely that sibling problems were part of a more general pattern of psychosocial and interpersonal difficulties, especially since sibling difficulties were a strong predictor of the security of the placements at a year, both for individual children and for the placements as a whole.

In the course of the report, we have already outlined some cases in which new parents reported high levels of antagonism and dispute between children. We have drawn attention to the manner in which these parents found this difficult to deal with and the way it reflected on their impressions of the children's settling in the home. Sometimes these interaction problems between children were extreme. One family who took two older boys spoke of the way in which the boys seemed to have very little time for each other. The younger child in particular was quite dismissive of the older one. The younger also had considerable behavioural problems including lying, stealing and disruptive behaviour at school. The boys' histories were characterised by neglect and parental inability to cope. Although they were capable of spending time together on occasion, the boys had frequent and extreme arguments resulting in fights that could end in physical injury. These fights could become so intense that the new mother felt unable to intervene without risking injury herself. Indeed, she reached a stage where she was frightened to be left alone with them when they were together because she felt unable to control them. Although sympathetic to the circumstances, the social worker in this case did not appear to appreciate the intensity of these problems and did not offer any help focused on this aspect of the placement.

In another case the new family had a group of three children, two girls and a boy, placed with them. The children had experienced sexual and emotional abuse as well as neglect. All three children engaged in frequent disputes and although their quarrels were not particularly violent, they were perpetual. They were consistently trying to get each other into trouble and displayed little positive interest in each other. The children did interact with their new parents appropriately and the placement seemed reasonably stable at the end of the year, but these new parents spoke of the physical and emotional exhaustion resulting from endless "refereeing".

Children's characteristics and experiences
Were there any factors in the children's histories that might have led to their difficulties? We explored the data on the family experiences the children had while with their birth families or earlier periods of care. Neither the children's biological relationships to each other, nor whether they had been together throughout their time in care, discriminated between a good and poorer approach to relationships. Factors like the stability of the birth family structure, the mobility of the family, parental discord or domestic violence were also unrelated to the quality of interaction between the children. Experiences of neglect, emotional and sexual abuse were not associated, although there were signs that physical abuse was more likely to be found in the histories of those with problems

Table 7.7
The proportion of children with parent interaction problems according to their sibling interaction at 3 and 12 months

	Number of children	Proportion with parent interaction problems	Significance
Sibling interaction at 3 months			
No problems	52	10%	n.s.
High conflict but caring	20	20%	
High conflict lacks care	13	31%	
Sibling interaction at 12 months			
No problems	51	12%	χ^2=6.0 (2) p=.049
High conflict but caring	16	6%	
High conflict lacks care	18	33%	

127

($\chi^2 = 5.2$, and 5.5 df= 2, p=.077 and .065 at three and 12 months respectively).

Children whose approach to siblings was characterised by high conflict and lack of care tended to be older at placement (F= 6.4 df= 2,98, p = .036). Lack of caring in particular was associated with older age at entry to care and older age at placement. These difficulties were not associated with the age gaps between children, spread of ages across the groups, or the birth order of the children.

There was an association between children's problems in their approach to siblings and their interaction with their new parents at the one year point, but it was by no means a perfect match (see Table 7.7). While there were some children who had difficulties approaching both their parents and siblings, there were several for whom only one type of relationship was problematic.

The differences at 12 months suggest that affectionless behaviour towards siblings is more strongly associated with problems in relationships with parents than conflict on its own.

Overview

In this chapter we have described the character of interaction between *groups of siblings*, examined relationships between *pairs of siblings* and explored the approach of *individual children* towards their siblings. Comparison with data from the general population group revealed that children placed with their siblings showed significantly more conflict and lower levels of warmth in their relationships than sibling pairs or groups that contained birth children of the current parents. Rivalry between children for parental attention was much more common in both joint and single placements than in the comparison group. Overall, there was substantial stability in the levels of conflict and rivalry over the course of the year although there were changes for some children and some groups.

The patterns of relationships among children in the comparison group generally agreed with other studies of sibling relationships in the general population. There tended to be less competition between children in mixed gender groups, in older sibling groups and in groups with a larger age spread. This pattern was not found among placed sibling groups where rivalry tended to occur across the board. Similarly, disputes between the children in these groups were a feature in all gender combinations. In the comparison group, conflict was more common among male pairs and groups where males predominated.

At the beginning of the year a disconcertingly high proportion of sibling groups were described as caring very little for each other. While this was understandable in the case of singly placed children with new siblings, it was more surprising among jointly placed children. By the end of the year, most of the new parents were reporting improvements in this feature for both types of placement although the changes were not dramatic.

Examination of the questionnaire data concentrated on the warmth and conflict scores for four different types of dyadic relationship: two placed children, one placed and one resident birth child, two resident birth children, and two comparison children. Major differences between jointly placed children and the other groups were once again found and the parent's ratings of these dyadic relationships did not suggest a substantial improvement in the degree of warmth or reduction in conflict between placed children over the course of the year.

Efforts to describe each of the individual children in terms of their approach to their siblings revealed that children who had problems in the way they related had significantly higher scores on measures of psychosocial problems. As a group they also had a higher mean age on admission to care, that is, they had spent longer in the care of their birth parents. There were no significant differences according to the experiences they had endured prior to leaving their family of origin, apart from a tendency for more physically abused children to have difficulties. Of course, children who had remained with their birth families longer may have experienced maltreatment for a longer period of time.

When we began the examination of parents' responses to the sibling relationship questionnaire, we noted that missing data at the one-year point might have meant that we were over-estimating the degree of conflict. It is also possible that previously child-free parents had little experience of children and over-emphasised normal squabbling. Parents of established families may have been particularly sensitive to the difficulties of their own or the placed children in adjusting to the new family structure. However, there are good reasons why the findings should be accepted. There was substantial agreement between question-naire and interview-based findings. The interview ratings were made on the basis of detailed parental accounts of relationships including blow-by-blow descriptions of disputes and their resolutions. On this basis the data can be taken as a good reflection of the way things were for these families. Potential differences in the parents' accounts that relate to their level of parenting experience are also important from a practice point of view because they reflect parents' problems and anxieties even if these differences present problems for data analysis and interpretation. Overall, a number of placed sibling groups showed no more difficulty in their relationships with each other than is true for most children. However, it is clear from the data that some parents need help and support and information on managing conflict, rivalry and lack of attachment among a substantial proportion of placed siblings as well as between placed children and their own birth children.

The findings concerning this last set of relationships, that is, between placed and birth children, deserve some comment. The data presented in this chapter show low levels of warmth and "connection" between the children and some rivalry for parental attention but not marked problems with disputes. How does this square with previous findings that place-ment with an "established" family was a risk factor? A number of points need to be made. First, these data apply only to the quality of the relationships between the children and not to the stability of placements as a whole. Secondly, the sample of children placed singly in established families was small and for this reason differences are harder to detect. Thirdly, the sibling group structures of the singly placed children in this sample are different from other studies. In particular, many of these single children became the youngest in their new family by a substantial margin. Finally, our earlier work suggested that the risks associated with placements in established families were indirect and involved a combina-tion of factors that included children's problems and parenting styles rather than the 'fact' of placement in an established family itself (Quinton et al, 1998).

This is not to say that placements with new siblings were without difficulties. Some of the birth children found it hard to adjust to the reality of placement, no matter how keen they had been initially on the idea of a new brother or sister. In the following chapter we explore the issues that arose for birth children and how these were addressed. Chapter 9 picks up the story for placed sibling groups and examines the extent of help that was offered to them and their new families.

KEY POINTS
The character of sibling relationships

- At the three-month point, the relationships among placed sibling groups were seen as predominantly positive in almost half the cases but parents saw no positive features at all in 22 per cent of placements.
- Rivalry and the frequency and severity of conflict and disputes were markedly elevated among placed sibling groups as against the comparison group.
- While the sibling relationships of many placed children were unremarkable, a substantial minority were problematic. For a small number the difficulties were extreme.
- The placements of children who showed a high conflict level in combination with a relative lack of care towards siblings were most likely to be classified as unstable at one year.
- Relationships between placed children and their new siblings (birth children of new parents) tended, in this sample, to be cool and somewhat distant but not conflicted. Reasons for the relative lack of problems were discussed.

---

8 The impact on the birth children

One of the ways in which fostering has differed broadly from adoption is that foster families have often incorporated children into an existing family, whereas children placed for adoption, at least in the past, were more likely to enter child-free families. Now that late placed children often enter families with resident birth children, the structure of adoptive and foster placements resemble each other much more.

Families applying to have children placed when they have already had children of their own may do so for a variety of reasons. For example, the children may have grown up and left home but the parents feel they have much to offer another child; or, where there are still children at home, medical reasons may prevent the birth of further children; or an altruistic decision might be made to take a child in need rather than have another of their own.

The early research into fostering highlighted the risks involved by moving a child into a home where there were already other children near in age (Parker, 1966). Surprisingly, this finding has not been explored in more detail. In particular, the response of the resident birth children to the incoming children has received little attention, although a few articles have addressed the question of the newly-created relationships (e.g. Nix, 1983). Thus, although the finding on the risk of breakdown in relation to the presence of birth siblings is well established, knowledge has not advanced very far beyond this.

Families with resident birth children
One purpose of this study was to understand more about the experiences of the birth children. In our sample, families with resident children formed a minority and this restricted our ability to examine the placements in detail and draw firm conclusions, but there were some general themes that may be helpful for practice.

Table 8.1 gives details of the numbers of resident children in the study.

In one family the combination of own and incoming children amounted to five.

Table 8.1
The placements containing resident children

Number of families with resident children	Number of resident children	Total resident birth children
8	1	8
7	2	14
2	3	6
Total 17		28

Impact on the birth children

We were able to assess the significance of the placement for the birth children from the initial discussions of the plan and through the first year of placement based on information from the parents and social workers. We asked about the initial reactions of the birth children: what proportion were seriously unsettled by the arrival of their new brothers or sisters; whether these reactions persisted; and whether there were positive as well as negative effects. We were also interested to know how the parents and the social work services responded when there were difficulties.

Initial reaction to the placement plan

We first asked the new parents to give their views on how each of their own children had reacted to the prospect of other children coming to join the family. Figure 8.1 shows that half the children were very keen on the plan but just under a third (8/28) had some reservations. In some families more than one child had reservations.

The children with reservations wondered about whether they would like the new children and be able to get along with them; how life would change; whether they would be happy to make certain compromises, like sharing a room to create space; and some wondered what it would be like to have a boy in the family for the first time. Seven of the

28 children living in the home were over 17 and it might be expected that they would have been able to take a more generous view of the placement plans. In fact this was not entirely the case. Three of them were not entirely supportive of the plan and expressed some jealous

Figure 8.1
The reaction of resident birth children to the placement plan

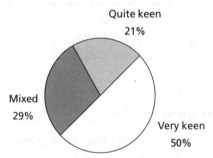

concerns.
Not surprisingly, some birth children who were initially keen on the plan were said at a year to be experiencing minor adjustment problems. No doubt the realities of communal living were impinging much more on them by that time. But, conversely, some who had a mixed initial reaction to the plan were said to have experienced little adverse effect once the incoming children arrived.

Impact on birth children during the first year
At both interview points we asked parents about the positive and negative impacts the placement had had on their birth children and how they had adapted to their new siblings. At the three-month point, the level of impact was fairly evenly spread: there had been little negative impact for 10 of the 28 birth children; minor adjustment problems for a further 12 of them; and more significant problems for the remaining six. Thus, 64 per cent were experiencing some kind of adjustment difficulty.

At one year, because of losses to the sample, information about the impact of placement was only available for 24 of the 28 birth children. Eight birth children appeared not to be having any problems but the proportion still having adjustment difficulties remained the same as at the three-month point (16/24; 67 per cent). In nine cases these were considered relatively minor hiccups in placements that were otherwise viewed positively, but there were more significant difficulties for seven young people. Interestingly, those identified as having problems in relation to the placement at the two time points were not necessarily the same: in the course of the year, difficulties settled for four of the original six children but developed for five others.

Despite the low numbers, it was possible to explore the experience of the birth children depending on their age at the time of the placement. The extent of problems was related to age in that the eight young people for whom there were no adjustment problems at a year tended to be adolescent.

A second question was whether the *age gap* between the resident and the placed children affected the level and kind of impact. Seven of the families (with 12 resident children) experienced moderate to severe impact. Three of the seven were placements that had a minimum age gap of less than three years, contrary to the practice advice, but the other four negative impact cases were in line with the guidance. Furthermore, in three of the 10 neutral impact cases, the practice advice had also been contravened. This suggests that although the recommendation regarding closeness in age should be adhered to if possible, following it does not confer immunity from problems.

Adapting to change
We asked what had helped the birth children to adapt to the changes. One factor that appeared to be important was the birth children's previous experiences of being a sibling. Eight of the 16 families who took part in the one year interview had two or more children of their own currently living at home (totalling 17 birth children). For the great majority of these children (13/17), the new parents felt that the opportunity to draw on their past experience of being a sibling and the chance to share the experience of placement with each other and to react together to the changes had been helpful. In addition, seven of the children were thought

to have drawn on other experiences which had helped them adapt. For example, some birth children had themselves experienced family disruption and loss and it is possible that this helped them to identify with the incoming children. In one case, there had been a great deal of social work intervention with the birth children directly to help with adjustment problems. The way the incoming child behaved and responded to the resident children and began to form relationships was described as a positive contribution in some cases; in other instances, their approach had led to friction and significant difficulties.

Non-resident birth children
We were also interested in those families where there were birth children who had grown up and no longer lived in the family, of whom there were 15. Although most accepted the placement plan, it was notable that three felt some jealousy. For example, one young woman, who had left home, was surprised to feel an uncomfortable sense of being on the margins of the newly created group. Seeing her former bedroom newly inhabited and family life changed resulted in some tense family disagreements. In other cases, the young people expressed concerns for their parents in taking on children with problems.

The impact on the birth children and parents' evaluation of placement

Of the 17 established families who took part in the study, only four evaluated the placement negatively and voiced significant ongoing concerns about its impact on their birth children.

Table 8.2
Negative impact on birth children at one year and the parents' evaluation of the placement

	Good evaluation	Poor evaluation	Total
Little or no impact	9	1	10
Moderate/severe impact	3	4	7

Table 8.2 shows that, where the impact on birth children was minimal, the placements were nearly all evaluated positively, but where the

negative impact was moderate or severe, over half of the placements were evaluated poorly by the parents despite the low numbers – these differences nearly reach the 5 per cent level of significance (exact probability 0.06). Nevertheless, it should be noted that some parents were able to take a positive view of the placements even when the impacts on their children were problematic, and also that parents could occasionally think that things were not going well even when their own children were not being adversely affected.

Relationships between parents and their own children
The quality of relationship between the parents and their own children at a year was described positively in all cases. Only one mother and two fathers felt that there were any problems in the attachment between them. None of the birth children were found to have psychosocial problems on the detailed interview questions nor were there any significant changes in these scores over the year.

Nevertheless, the parents did report more subtle changes in their children. For eight youngsters these changes were in a negative direction, while there were improvements in six children. These changes occurred across a range of areas and are listed in Table 8.3. For the most part, negative changes were attributed to reaching adolescence rather than to the effect of the placement itself. Reasons for positive changes were evenly spread between explanations of increasing age or maturity, growing comfort with the new family constellation, and the way the parents were dealing with specific problems.

Table 8.3
Changes in birth children

Area of change	Deterioration	Improvement
Openness/affection	13%	4%
Behaviour	17%	4%
Academic performance	8%	0%
Emotional	0%	4%
New sibling relationships	8%	17%

Social worker perceptions of new sibling issues in placement

Social workers reported difficulties for the new sibling arising during introductions for only one of the 17 placements, but by the three-month point, they were seeing moderate to considerable problems in 25 per cent of placements. In almost all cases, parents were thought to be dealing with the difficulties appropriately.

Social workers' reports usually, but not always, agreed with the parents' views. There was agreement that significant problems between the children were present at one year for five of the seven placements where the parents reported difficulties. Conversely, there were three families where practitioners had been concerned about the impact on the resident birth children but where the new parents said that these difficulties were either balanced by positive features of the placement or had resolved by the 12-month interview.

As shown in Table 8.4, sibling difficulties had been noted by social workers in nearly half the families (eight of 17 cases) during the course of the year. They were of sufficient magnitude for them to feel that they contributed to parents' feelings of doubt about the longer term viability of the placement in four of these. Doubts were less likely to have been discussed with social workers in the absence of new sibling relationship problems.

Table 8.4

Social workers' perceptions of parental doubt about placement viability according to level of new sibling relationship difficulties

New sibling problems	Degree of doubt about viability of placement as reported by social workers		
	None	Brief periods	Frequent or constant
None or only minor	7	2	
Moderate or considerable	1	3	4

Social work help with sibling relationships

Social workers said parents had asked for help about issues concerning these new siblings in six of these eight cases, but substantial amounts of work directly involving the young people were noted for only three of them. In one case, work was done with the whole family in an attempt to help with the difficulties, and the birth children had direct social work help in the other two cases.

Overview

We began this chapter by emphasising that the number of placements involving incoming children joining resident birth children was low and this limited the amount of statistical analysis that was possible. Nevertheless, it is increasingly recognised that birth children of substitute carers are important participants at all stages of placement and neither their influence on the progress of the placement nor the impact upon them should be ignored.

Social workers said that parents asked for help over sibling relationships in six cases but this was provided in a way that involved the children themselves in only three instances. There are clearly questions arising from this concerning the preparedness of both new parents and social workers for work of this nature to be undertaken directly with birth children.

Parents felt that while there were hurdles to be cleared regarding minor jealousies and disruption of previous family routines, most of the birth children had experienced the first year of placement as a positive event. However, in a minority of cases, tensions and jealousies arose even for the adult children of the new families. We found no clear pattern in the minority of cases where parents reported more significant problems to suggest which placements may be at greatest risk. For example, the age gap between the incoming and resident children had some impact but the effect was not striking. Indeed, there were placements that progressed very well despite closeness in age and some that did less well where the recommendations were followed. We concluded that the policy of placing with a three year age gap is a useful guide for practitioners, but that difficulties can occur even when this is followed. There is a need for careful and thorough preparation of all birth children and a mechanism by which they can get help when they wish.

KEY POINTS
The impact on the birth children

- Most of the birth children experienced the arrival of the new children as a positive event but there were tensions and jealousies for a minority.
- Half the birth children were keen on the placement plan initially but some of these later had adjustment problems.
- Some birth children who had left home felt jealousy about the new family that had been created.

---

9 Social work intervention with siblings placed together

Chapter 7 drew attention to high levels of conflict and rivalry among the children placed together. In this chapter we look in more detail at the types of problem and the ways in which the social workers responded to the needs of the children and families.

Social workers thought that the children in 27 of the 40 sibling group placements had difficult relationships, although these difficulties were seen as marked in only 12 cases. In the analyses of social work actions that follow we concentrate primarily on these placements. However, it seems likely that the social workers' evaluations underestimate the level of sibling difficulties. In the interviews, the social workers were inclined to interpret emotional and behavioural problems as the difficulties of individual children rather than to see some of them as relationship conflicts. The new parents reported seriously problematic relationships more frequently than social workers (16 out of 40 placements).

In three of the 12 cases identified by social workers as experiencing marked sibling difficulties, no service or very little service was being provided. These parents had to rely on their own resources. In one case they were not prepared to proceed to adoption without better support and this resulted in legal delays in securing the placement for the children.

The remaining nine cases received more substantial and more targeted help. In addition to the routine visiting – fortnightly or monthly – of the family social workers (FSWs), help was either directed at the siblings themselves or to enable the parents to manage the sibling relationship difficulties. It was usual for the more intensive work to be carried out by the FSWs but occasionally the children's social workers (CSWs) conducted the direct work with the children because they often knew them well. In the other two cases, the social workers saw their role as securing a specialist referral and then liaising with the agency.

Much of the intensive help by the FSW consisted of reviewing with the parents the possible causes of the sibling conflict. For example, in one case the phenomenon of the "parental child" was explained and, in another, the possible impact of the changing age structure of a family when siblings are placed with resident children was discussed. Advice, when given, tended to be at the level of general management principles rather than through promoting specific techniques or strategies. However, there were some examples of new parents being urged to find ways of helping children who were locked into conflict to become more separate in their activities and friendships.

Some more detailed case examples follow, illustrating more focused interventions but with differing outcomes. In some cases, this work led to clear benefits for the families and the children, but in other cases even very intensive work failed to resolve the difficulties within the first year of placement. In a minority of cases, these problems were influential in the disruption of the placement.

Intervention and positive benefit

The first example concerns the placement of a sibling pair. The older girl was jealous of her younger brother: she bullied him and was destructive towards his possessions. The FSW made a referral to the Child and Adolescent Mental Health Service for individual therapy for the older girl. Regular, direct work was provided with the clear objective of encouraging her to examine her behaviour towards her brother and to find more constructive ways of dealing with her wish to dominate him. The girl became very involved in the work and found it helpful. The FSW assisted the parents in establishing clear limits as to what was acceptable. The bullying lessened and there was general agreement that a noticeable and positive difference had occurred in her behaviour.

The siblings in the second case had been separated for two years and reunited in the permanent placement. They had a history of mutual hostility and intense conflict and both felt they were not receiving equal parental attention. The CSW gave advice on handling sibling relationships that was informed by her detailed knowledge of the children's histories. The new parents found this helpful and the rivalry abated during the year.

Another case with a positive outcome involved a specialist referral where anger management techniques were offered to two physically aggressive boys. The local authority gave generous support for extra resources. Major improvements in the boys' strategies for managing conflicts were shown over the year. It was agreed that the additional help had been invaluable and that, despite initial problems, this remained the right placement for them.

Intervention and continuing instability

The case illustrated under this heading had been marked by a difference of opinion amongst social workers as to whether joint placement was the best plan and the disagreements continued regarding what level of difficulty was tolerable in placement. (These differences in social work opinion were noted in the research when comparing the same question across separate interviews.) Two brothers were described as having difficulty communicating effectively with each other. Each had intense individual needs and problems that led to sibling squabbles and physical fights that constituted the worse aspect of the placement for the new parents. Intensive visits supported the new parents but the FSW continued to wonder whether the boys might have been better placed singly. However, the CSW was convinced that no other family could have responded to the children's needs as well as their present parents, nor succeeded in keeping them together. The FSW was more aware of the substantial sibling conflicts and the effect on the new parents, whereas the CSW was either less aware of, or less concerned by, the level of group conflict. There was disagreement between the family and the CSW who was eventually asked to withdraw. By the one-year point, plans to arrange extra help had faltered and the mother was trying independently to arrange advice from a psychologist to reduce the constant conflicts.

The next case illustrates weekly direct work by the CSW with two boys who were persistently aggressive, verbally and physically, to each other. The interactions of the boys with each other and with their new mother were observed. The boys were very different: the older boy was more stable and academically inclined and the younger immature and dreamy. The mother related more easily to the older boy. When the placement reached crisis point, the parents requested removal of the boys but subsequently relented. However, more intensive efforts to work directly with the children were not regarded by the new mother as sufficiently effective. At one year, the placement continued to be unstable with the possibility of further, separate placements being considered. The new parents were withdrawing from the boys in the face of their constant wrangling, arousing concern that they were no longer meeting their needs.

Intervention and disruption

In one case friction between two boys was so great that the new parents resorted to pulling them apart physically, sometimes making parent–child relations worse in the process. The FSW tried to offer alternative strategies, but to little effect as the parents had begun to dislike the children. The CSW arranged sessions with the boys to continue with life story work. Despite poor concentration, they started to make use of the sessions. Nevertheless the placement hit further crises and eventually broke down. Since then, in their separate placements, neither boy has been reported as presenting a problem. The social workers, in the light of this, concluded that this should always have been the placement plan.

Parents' concerns and social work responses

As mentioned earlier, there was generally good agreement between the social work and parent reports of sibling relationship problems, although there was some variation in the degree of importance that each party attached to these difficulties. However, there was a worrying variation in the extent to which some social workers responded to these problems. There were a few workers (7) who reported that they had discussed the nature of the sibling relationships with the parents although the parents were not reporting marked problems. These workers were clearly approaching the support task in a thorough manner and taking a proactive stance. However, there were eight families who were reporting significant problems in the relationships between their children. In these cases, the social workers had not undertaken any specific work or referred the family to any other resource.

In three of these cases the parents were reporting marked sibling difficulties to the research interviewer. However, it may be that these problems were not being discussed with the social workers as sibling problems but as individual behaviour problems. In another three cases, the new parents' own professional experience of children may have led to the social workers themselves feeling their contributions were less valuable. The remaining two cases represented an inadequate social work response.

Approaches to intervention

Much of what we recorded as intensive help involved separate work with parents and children. It was noticeable that family systems thinking was never explicitly mentioned in the context of relationships in the newly created family. Such a model may have helped to create a fuller picture of the emerging pattern of relationships. Furthermore, the families may have profited from sharing their experiences of being a new family struggling jointly with their problems.

It is not possible from case examples to assess with certainty the effect of social work and other interventions on troublesome sibling relationships. For example, in the cases of positive outcome it was impossible to say whether it was the intervention itself, the efforts of the parents, the passage of time, or a combination of factors that made the difference. In cases of more negative outcomes, intensive efforts may merely have been trailing after crises in placements destined to fail.

The literature on preparation of children for placement places heavy stress on seeking the children's views. Such an approach should also continue post placement to see how the children view their new family environment. What appears to be informing the children's problem behaviour? How do they understand their sibling history? Why do they think they are together now or, perhaps, why were they separated in the past? How are their expectations of relationships being fulfilled now that they have moved? Continuing engagement with the children as well as the parents will provide fuller information on the children's viewpoint which should help practitioners to select the most appropriate type of intervention.

The social workers were clearly faced with difficult decisions in making the placement plan and, as was clear from the examples, in deciding what action to take if the plans were not working out well. We suggest that social workers take particular care to think beyond received imperatives and consider what really justifies a placement plan. This would require thinking about the *quality* of the sibling relationship and having at their disposal the concepts to describe and assess the nature of interactions and to think through *the consequences for relationships* of their decisions. The capacity to be alert to relationship problems is essential for developing a better grasp of the range of challenges confronting the new parents.

The fact that sibling relationship difficulties were found to be associated both with placement instability for individual children and with new parents' overall evaluation of the placement, makes it imperative that sibling considerations are given higher priority. Appropriate support and funding for specialist help need to be available, should it prove necessary, and wherever pre-placement assessment indicates the desirability of joint placement but where problems nevertheless are anticipated.

KEY POINTS
Social work intervention with
siblings placed together

- Advice on sibling relationship difficulties, when given by social workers, tended to be at the level of general management principles rather than through promoting specific techniques or strategies.
- Intensive help usually took the form of separate interventions for parents and children rather than work with the whole family.

---

10 Summary and implications

As with any research, there are limits to what can be accomplished and limits to what can be concluded. When we set out on this study, we made a deliberate choice to base the study on face-to-face interviews since this method provides much richer data that can be more easily clarified with the respondent than is true of self completed questionnaires. It also meant that we could be confident of the representativeness of the sample. This choice, however, necessarily limited the size of the sample. Although the statistical tests used take the small group sizes into account, there have been occasions in the course of this report when we have had to abandon further analyses because the groupings became too small for tests to be reliable. However, had we been struggling with less rich data, the questions we were trying to tackle may never have come to light. We believe, therefore, that the interview method was correct in this circumstance, despite its drawbacks, in order for more complex associations to be revealed.

In Chapter 2 we outlined our aims in conducting this study, which were as follows:

- To study social work decisions about separation, reunion or maintenance of the sibling group.
- To investigate the location, circumstances and contact arrangements of birth siblings who were not with the placed children.
- To examine placement outcomes for individual children of similar age according to whether they were placed with or without siblings.
- To explore the character of relationships between children in different types of placement (child-free or established families).
- To examine the sibling relationships of children placed together from care in comparison with those of children growing up in their own families.
- To examine the impact of placement on the resident birth children of the new families.
- To document the level and type of social work intervention with particular reference to sibling relationships.

We first summarise what we have been able to establish in relation to each of these aims. We then move on to consider in more detail one very important outstanding question.

Making decisions about the placement of children with siblings

The first point to make in relation to this aspect of the study is that while 80 per cent of the sample had other siblings, only one-third of them had siblings who were elsewhere in the care system. For the majority of both singletons and sibling groups, the move to the new home represented a continuation of previous placement arrangements. There was evidence, in the majority of cases, that a good deal of thought had been given to the constellations in which children would join their permanent family: indeed in six of the sibling group placements children had been reunited for this placement.

Reasons for separation

Among the relatively small group of children who had siblings who were looked after elsewhere, the reasons given for separation differed according to whether the permanent placement was one of a single child or a sibling group. Children whose sibling/s were also looked after but were nevertheless entering their new placement alone had almost always been separated because of the social worker's view that their individual needs would be best met by a singleton placement. Such judgements were usually due to the difficult behaviour of one or more of the siblings or because of problematic interaction between the children. Behavioural difficulties have repeatedly been shown to threaten the stability of placements and it is clear from this study that enduring problems between siblings negatively affect the new parents' satisfaction with the placement. In most cases, although the separation had frequently been quite longstanding, reunion was considered carefully while planning the permanent placement of those who were placed alone.

In contrast, while some of those placed jointly were separated from other siblings because of individual needs (54 per cent), there were nearly as many who were separated from other siblings because they entered care at different times (46 per cent). The possibility of reunion was rarely considered for this latter group. This might initially seem to suggest that there were some splintered sibling groups whose possible reunion was receiving little social work attention. However, in practice the groups that were separated because they entered care at different times, tended to be half-siblings to those placed, and there were frequently large age gaps between the two sets of children

While it could be argued that age gaps or biological relationships are less important than the opportunity to grow up with brothers and sisters, reunion in these circumstances would create large sibling groups with a wide age spread. Many of these children would not have lived together for many years. These characteristics would make it difficult to find a family with the space, skills and time to care for such a group as well as presenting problems in securing the financial and material support to make the placement possible.

We would not wish to underestimate the difficulties and dilemmas involved in planning permanent placements, but the need to achieve permanence may in some cases be in competition with the aim of keeping siblings together. This is evidenced in those cases where separation had been a reasoned choice resulting from the behavioural problems of one or other sibling or the relationships between them. Reconciling the aims of permanence and maintenance of siblings together is likely to require a greater emphasis on improving the behaviour of children or the relationships between them at an earlier point in their care careers thereby reducing the need for the initial separation. Of course, this might itself entail a wider use of other professional resources.

It was clear that most of the separations of children occurred some time before permanence plans were being considered and in some cases happened purely because of different dates of reception into care. While there are limitations to the numbers of children that can be placed with any one family, it might be possible to establish placements with an agreement between the authority and carers for further children from the same family to be placed later.

The children's contact with siblings elsewhere

The importance of contact between separated siblings, in both the short and longer term, is yet to be systematically addressed by research. However, evidence from a study on the Adoption Contact Register (Mullender and Kearne, 1997), although based on a self-selected sample, suggests that having lost contact with siblings can have extremely important consequences for individuals later in life. In the absence of evidence to the contrary, it seems reasonable to proceed cautiously and aim for maintenance of contact with siblings wherever this is possible.

As indicated above, the great majority of the children had at least one sibling living elsewhere. Overall, we found that half the placements were made without any plan for sibling contact. Meetings were more likely if the other siblings were also looked after rather than living with birth parents. But even in this group there was a very evident decline in the extent to which social workers anticipated that contact between the siblings would continue after the move to the permanent placement.

Interestingly, most of the children who had been in contact with siblings in the past would continue to see at least some of their brothers and sisters, but they were to stay in touch with fewer of them. The reason for the reduction in the extent of sibling contact at the point of permanent placement was not at all clear from the data available. Over the course of the first year of placement, meetings with siblings tended to take place as planned.

Our discussions with new families suggested that, on the whole, they were very open to facilitating contact with siblings, although there were practical issues to be considered, especially where siblings were placed in a number of different locations. Although it may not always be possible to maintain ideal contact conditions in emergency or short-term placements, when matching children for permanence, consideration must be given to where separated siblings are placed and how contact between them can best be ensured.

In the study there were examples of new families who had succeeded in establishing very friendly relationships with the families caring for their children's siblings. Contact visits were relaxed and informal and occurred largely within the normal pattern of visits with the extended family. Equally, there were cases where new parents had found a good deal of resistance from the other carers, both custodial birth parents and adoptive or foster families. This could happen where the "other sibling/s" had been placed for some time and their families were anxious to avoid any disturbance to the placement. If severing of ties is to be avoided, it is crucial that all those caring for children who have siblings, birth families, foster families and prospective adopters are aware of the importance of maintaining some sibling links.

In a few cases (13 per cent) new parents voiced reservations about contact and felt that it had a somewhat negative effect on their children. This tended to occur when the contact exposed the children to undesirable behaviour or lifestyles or where the children were actually frightened of their brothers or sisters. Although relatively rare among this sample, the reasons behind these reservations highlight the fact that it is not sufficient simply to establish contact arrangements. Ensuring that contact arrangements are positive for all concerned entails active social work involvement with all those participating at the setting up stage and continued availability of social work assistance should circumstances change.

It was evident that there was even less contact when siblings remained with the birth family. Although in some cases birth parents may not wish to retain contact, even indirectly, with their children, the need for both the children who have left and those that remain to have knowledge of each other should be considered. For children of an appropriate age who remain with the birth family, it may be worth establishing their individual views on keeping in touch with their sibling/s.

We concentrated on face-to-face meetings between children and their siblings, largely because there were so few examples of other means of contact. While there may be occasions when direct contact between siblings may be thought inadvisable, perhaps for reasons of confidentiality or concerns about an abusive sibling relationship, there was surprisingly little use of indirect means of contact. The children in our study were mostly of an age to be able to appreciate some form of written communication and certainly old enough to talk to siblings on the phone. However, while cards were exchanged and phone calls made when there was also face-to-face contact, these methods were rarely employed as a sole means of allowing children to stay in touch with their brothers and sisters. These more indirect methods may be worth considering when direct contact is not deemed advisable. Contact between separated siblings requires considerable social work attention much earlier in the process. Nearly half the sample had lost contact with their brothers and sisters prior to plans being made to find them a permanent family.

Placement outcomes

A total of seven of the 72 placements disrupted in the course of the first year, including two sibling groups and five singly placed children. However, beyond the bald fact of the disruption rate, it was evident that there was variation in the ease with which children had become part of their new family. Our exploration of one-year outcomes therefore concentrated on the extent to which *individual* children had settled with the new family and the way in which new parents evaluated placements from a *whole family* perspective. We found that most of these permanent placements progressed well in the course of the first year. Four-fifths (100 of 125) of the individual children placed settled well with their new families and developed relationships that satisfied the new parents. From the family perspective, parents in 53 of 72 placements (74 per cent) reported that the year had been at least balanced in terms of challenges and rewards, and on the whole it had been an experience they valued and would not wish to change.

There were no significant differences in one-year outcome according to whether the children had siblings from whom they were separated, for either singly or jointly placed children.

There was a tendency for a larger proportion of singleton placements to be in the poorer outcome group at a year (38 per cent as opposed to 18 per cent). This is in line with previous studies, which have shown varied outcomes but with a leaning towards evidence of better progress for sibling placements. However, it is likely that singly and jointly placed children are not directly comparable. The characteristics of the children and their reasons for coming to placement on their own or with siblings need to be examined in order to understand this finding. Practitioners faced with difficult placement choices about maintaining or separating sibling groups may greet our main findings with some perplexity. We did find a small advantage in favour of sibling placement, although this was not unequivocal. The implication of the finding is that practitioners should maintain a positive view of sibling group placement, but must assess, on a case-by-case basis, whether particular concerns might argue for a different decision. According to the evidence, it is not possible routinely to prescribe one placement choice over another. When we looked closely at how this might be explained, we found, as we discuss below, that there were important ways in which the pre-placement backgrounds for the sibling groups differed from those of singletons. The placement decision must therefore involve careful consideration of the challenges inherent in the singly placed child's relationship with parents or carers and a similar consideration of the challenges inherent in sibling group relationships.

When exploring what may have led to difficulties in those cases where outcomes were classified as poorer, some interesting differences emerged. For both singly and jointly placed children, difficulties in their interaction patterns, either with parents or siblings, were found to be associated with negative parental evaluations of the placement. It should be noted that "child–parent interaction difficulties" were defined as quite specific features of the children's behaviour towards the parent figure (see Chapter 6). However, as outlined below, these interaction difficulties were associated with different factors for singly and jointly placed children.

Factors associated with placement outcome for singly placed children

For children placed alone, an experience of having been rejected by the birth family increased the risk both of poorer placement stability and of difficult interaction patterns with new parents. The children classified as rejected were significantly more likely to resist affection from the start of placement, to be somewhat inappropriate in the affection that they did show and to fail to differentiate their new parents from other adults. These problems persisted and by the end of the year they were less likely than non-rejected children to show spontaneous affection to their new parents.

This, in turn, was associated with the new parents' perceptions of

153

whether the children were settled in placement and their level of doubt about continuing with the placement. The findings concerning the link between relationship problems and poorer outcomes confirm those of other studies in the field which have examined the child's integration with the new family (Nelson, 1985; Hodges and Tizard, 1989). The additional finding that this pattern of behaviour is particularly likely to be found among children who have been in some way singled out or rejected by their birth parents has important implications for those working with such children or planning for their care. It is impossible to say from this study whether these children's difficulties can be success-fully resolved through direct work prior to placement. However, the findings suggest that it is crucial that new families are prepared for these children to experience difficulties in building new relationships with parent figures.

Within this sample, the presence of the new parents' birth children was not strongly related to outcome, as has been the case in other studies. There were examples of very difficult placements where new siblings were involved, but these were relatively few and balanced by placements in which progress was good. There was no clear pattern in relation to age gaps, or any other factors, which were associated with the quality of new sibling relationships. In a previous study we found a history of rejection to be associated with poor relationships with new siblings; however, most of the rejected children in this study joined child-free families and it was not possible to explore this further.

The lack of differential outcome according to the presence or absence of birth children suggests that the differences previously found are probably due to variations across studies in terms of which families take on what kinds of children, rather than to any intrinsic problems with established family placements. Likewise, the relatively high level of poor outcomes among children placed on their own in child-free families implies that the difficulties that some children bring with them may be hard to deal with, even for families who can concentrate their attention and effort on one child. That said, our group of placements with estab-lished families was very small. Therefore, although it is clear that these placements can work out well, there is certainly no evidence from this study to challenge the current practice guidance of proceeding with caution and trying to ensure sufficient age gaps between resident and placed children.

Factors associated with placement outcome for jointly placed children

There were relatively few instances of poor one-year outcomes among jointly placed children (15 i.e. 16 per cent). It was striking that the association between singling out or rejection and poorer outcomes was not apparent for children placed with their siblings. These children did not show raised levels of problems in getting on with their new parents. There seemed no doubt that these jointly placed children had been singled out for negative parental attention in their birth families, but their experiences were necessarily different from children who were rejected and alone in leaving their family of origin. The psychological mechanisms that to some extent protected these children are not known, but the sense of rejection might have been lessened by the *shared* experience of leaving the family home.

Where poorer settling in and difficulties in relating to parents occurred, they were more common among those who had been sexually or physically abused. Difficulties between siblings were also significantly associated with poorer outcomes.

Children who were reported to have difficulties in their interaction with their siblings were not necessarily scoring highly on our scale of child–parent interaction problems. This suggests that new parents may well find it more difficult to bond with children who have difficulty interacting with their siblings, regardless of the way in which the children behave towards them. Certainly there was anecdotal evidence from new parents that they found it hard to view some of the more outrageous behaviours towards siblings with a neutral eye. With this in mind, it is essential that practitioners are attuned to the possibilities of significant difficulties between children, that these are not under-played when they are reported, and that appropriate help is forthcoming.

The children's relationships with their siblings

We examined children's relationships with each other from a variety of viewpoints including a comparison with sibling pairs in the general population. Increased levels of rivalry for the parents' attention compared with the comparison families were a feature of sibling placements and placements of single children into families with resident birth children.

Relationships between siblings placed together

The analyses presented in Chapter 7 showed that jointly placed children exhibited greater levels of conflict and, in the early months at least, less warmth than was true for children in the general population. Parents of placed sibling groups in particular were identifying and worrying about high levels of conflict between their children. The existence of sibling relationship difficulties had an impact on the parents' perception of the placement as a whole and the extent to which the placements of the children, looked at individually, were stable in the longer term.

In Chapter 7 we saw that problems in relationships with siblings were more likely where children had entered care at an older age and that conflict was more likely for the older children in a sibling group. On the other hand, there was no evidence that particular *types* of abuse or other adverse experiences within the family of origin were significantly implicated in poorer sibling relationships.

In Chapter 9 we examined the social work response to these problems. In most cases, social workers were aware of these difficulties but the degree of importance they attached to them was inadequate in some cases. There were relatively few examples of specialist help being enlisted to improve sibling relationships and the direct work provided by practitioners tended to focus on parents and children separately. There is currently little guidance or training available to social workers needing to help children in their relationships with brothers and sisters and it is clear that this is a crucial area of practice.

Relationships between placed children and resident birth children

The number of placements that involved resident birth children were very small and this necessarily limited the analyses that could be undertaken. Not surprisingly, the level of warmth between the placed and birth children was low early on in the placement. By the end of the year, although relations were still relatively cool, most parents felt that they were developing appropriately. There were very low levels of conflict, doubtless influenced by the fact that many of the birth children were in their middle teenage years. However, it is also possible that the low conflict coupled with low warmth may be indicative of a distant relationship rather than a balanced one. Although not characterised by overt disagreements, there was a high level of mutual rivalry between placed children and their new siblings.

Our exploration of the more subtle features of new sibling placements in Chapter 8 revealed that most of the birth children were reported to have experienced the first year of placement as a primarily positive event. However, there had frequently been minor jealousies and disruption of family routines and, in a minority of cases, the placement had a more significant impact on the birth children. There were no clear predictors of which placements might be at risk of more serious difficulties. Even though age appeared to be a factor – with older birth children having fewer problems than younger ones – there were a few cases in which tensions and jealousies were encountered with adult birth children.

Following the placement rule of a minimum three-year gap between the youngest birth child and the placed child is a useful guide, but practitioners need to be aware that difficulties can occur even when this rule is followed. The extent to which placed and previously resident children are able, over time, to view each other as siblings remains an unexplored area. With one or two notable exceptions, there was surprisingly little evidence of practitioners working directly with the birth children, either in the preparatory phase or following placement, even though the ages of the birth children would have allowed for some discussion with them about their hopes, fears and experiences.

Outstanding questions

There is one key question, which was not among our study aims but which nevertheless requires some consideration. This concerns the preference to be given to maintaining or reuniting a sibling group because of the assumed merits of growing up together as against the importance of stability, continuity and attachment with caregivers. We know from our post bag that these concerns can severely exercise practitioners. There are cases of potential reunion when placement together may mean uprooting a child from another placement and breaking a significant attachment. There are also cases where maintaining a sibling group may mean moving all children when it is only one child who has not settled in a placement. Other circumstances may mean running a risk of upsetting a placement that is stable by introducing another child from the family.

Do data from our study contribute anything to this debate? Sadly they do not. Our study was not designed to answer this question. We collected our data at the point that *new* permanent placements had been arranged because our focus was on the initial adjustment of the children in their new families. A study designed to address this debate would have to follow up children with siblings elsewhere where the decision was that they should remain in the same placement and to compare them with children transferred to a new family to be with their siblings.

Such a study would involve substantial methodological problems, particularly with regard to establishing equivalence in the children to start with. Decisions about the placement of children are not made randomly and practitioners already employ their best judgement about the best interests of the children. Therefore, it is likely in this hypothetical study design that those who left long-standing carers to be re-united with siblings would have a different quality of relationship with those carers, and probably with their estranged siblings, than would be true of those who stayed with the current carers. However, if this were possible and the majority of the sample could be studied at various follow-up points, a more definitive answer could be given.

Lacking such a study at present, we can only consider what evidence there is on the consequences of either option. There is now a sufficient body of evidence on the negative consequences of broken attachments to say that this is to be avoided if at all possible, as long as this is in other ways consistent with the child's welfare (Howe, 1996). There is a much smaller body of evidence on the developmental consequences of discontinuity of sibling relationships. Our literature review in Chapter 1 indicates that such separations can be painful and the effects are sometimes of long duration, although the consequences may not be as extensive and profound as the known consequences for adult psychological adjustment of early parent–child separations. On this basis, it could be argued that more weight should therefore be given to preserving the secure parent–child attachment. However, we simply do not know what proportion of those separated from their siblings experience substantial and lasting adverse effects.

The voice that is unheard in our study is that of the children. Because of the newness of the placements and the relatively young ages of many of the sample, it was not felt appropriate to introduce the added complication of research interviews into the children's lives. There is, however, clearly a need for independent research to address children's views about living with or apart from their brothers and sisters, although interpretation of the findings would have to be tempered by considering the likelihood of their views changing with age and maturity. We know that sibling relationships can go through periods of substantial difficulty but nevertheless become an important source of support later in life.

Conclusions

We feel confident in concluding that, in the majority of cases, guidance in relation to sibling placements was being followed and that social workers considered children's siblings when they were planning for them. However, it was clear that the twin principles of achieving permanence and maintaining siblings together were at times operating in competition with each other. Achieving both would clearly place a far greater demand on resources. What appeared to be missing from the equation was the degree to which growing up with siblings was viewed as a legitimate need comparable to the need for stability through permanence. As we have discussed, the research necessary to answer this question has yet to be undertaken. In the meantime, the available evidence suggests that secure attachments to long-standing carers should not be disturbed unduly.

There was room for considerable improvement in the arrangements made to promote ongoing contact between separated children. This was especially true for those whose siblings remain with the birth family. Many new parents were happy to consider and implement contact, although support may well be required. More research is needed into the different types of contact and their effects.

This study has found no evidence that sibling placements fare worse than those of children placed on their own. Indeed, if anything, the data are in line with many other studies that show sibling placements to be associated with greater stability, at least in the short term. However, for reasons we have discussed, it would be premature to conclude that the greater problems of singly placed children would have been lessened had they been placed with siblings.

The study has been able to confirm that, for both sibling and singleton placements, the difficulties in the integration of children into their new families were strongly related to the children's styles of interaction both with each other and with parent figures. In this study, the patterns of interaction between the children were not related to the parenting approaches.

Further research needs to concentrate on understanding relationships in new placements. Problems in these areas seem more influential on the course of placements and may be more resistant to change than other features of emotional and behavioural development. Methodological developments coming from attachment theory are a likely starting point but these need to be developed to encompass sibling relationships from an attachment perspective and not just as a feature of parent–child relationships.

It was hardly a surprise to find that the relationships between children who need permanent placement were more problematic than relationships among birth siblings in the general population. Nevertheless, the extent and severity of these problems need to be recognised. Poor relationships between siblings were often the reason for separation of children in care, but poor relationships were also apparent for many children placed together. While there were cases of social work intervention specifically directed at these problems during the course of the first year, concern for sibling relationships was quite low on the agenda of social workers in both preparation and post-placement support. If future separation of children is to be avoided, it is clear that much more attention to relationships is required at a much earlier stage in care careers.

New developments and afterthoughts

Since preparing the initial version of this report, much has happened in children and families social work and with regard to permanent place- ment in particular. The new *Framework for the Assessment of Children in Need and their Families* (DoH, 2000) draws attention to the importance of observing and assessing family and social relationships, beyond that of parent/s and child. We are aware that we have been quite critical in some cases of the depth of assessment applied to one of the most serious and long-lasting decisions that may be made for children. It was also evident from the study that, although not articulated as such, there were circumstances when the personal views of practitioners regarding separation or maintenance were driving the decision-making. We are aware that established guidance in this regard has been a long time coming. The DoH in 1991 published a checklist to help practitioners consider whether children were best placed together or apart. Our research suggests that this has not been widely adopted. Although a minority of authorities in our study had developed their own format for assessment and some interviewees mentioned the DoH checklist, a number of practitioners responded to our question about structured assessment with an astonished 'is there such a thing?'.

As we write, we are aware that BAAF (British Agencies for Adoption and Fostering) following consultation, is preparing a new good practice guide (Lord and Borthwick, 2001, forthcoming) which draws together the main research findings concerning the placement of children with siblings. We hope that, when it becomes available, it will provide a useful basis from which local authority managers and practitioners can develop more uniform practice, based on a comprehensive assessment of children's placement and/or contact needs in relation to their brothers and sisters. In our view, sibling considerations certainly need to be brought to the fore in all areas of placement practice.

We trust that it will be possible in time to learn more about how important growing up with siblings really is and that practice will continue to develop in light of the research findings yet to come. Meanwhile, there are three important messages from this piece of research. The first is that, in some cases, specialised work with children and carers may be required to reduce the need for the initial separation of siblings. Secondly, prospective families for sibling groups need to anticipate the possibility of higher than average levels of rivalry and conflict. Preparation and support for the placement should consider how these may be contained and how more positive sibling interaction might be encouraged. Finally, it is likely that there will always be some circumstances in which it is necessary or desirable to place children apart from each other. However, there are likely to be few cases in which cessation of contact between them is justified. A clear need exists to improve planning and management of contact between separated children.

The driving force behind this study has been to contribute to practice knowledge about making and supporting the permanent placement of children who have brothers and sisters, whether or not they are placed together. The outcomes we have examined in this report are limited to the way in which the children settled over their first year, knowledge of which is crucial for planning placement support. What is needed now is a longer-term perspective, which will allow us to discover whether the tendency for singleton placements to progress less smoothly persists over time and indeed whether sibling groups, progressing well in middle childhood, continue to do so into adolescence and beyond.

KEY POINTS
Summary and implications

Separation of siblings
- There was evidence of a good deal of thought being given to keeping siblings together.
- Separation of singly placed children was usually because of individual needs.

- The initial separation had usually occurred some years before the permanent placement.

Contact with siblings

- Half the placements were made without any plan for sibling contact.
- Contact with siblings was viewed positively by the families, but is likely to require ongoing social work involvement.
- There was very little use of indirect means of contact between separated siblings.

Placement outcomes

- Around three-quarters of placements were classified as satisfactory or good outcome at a year.
- Poorer outcome was more common for singly placed children, but singly and jointly placed children were not directly comparable.
- An experience of rejection by birth parents increased the risk of poor outcome for singly placed children. Rejected children who were placed with siblings were not at increased risk of poor placement outcome.
- The presence of birth children in the new family was not related to outcome, but this group was very small and may have been atypical.
- Factors most strongly related to placement stability were children's interaction style with both new parents and each other.

Sibling relationships

- Rivalry between children was a feature of both types of placement.
- As a group, siblings placed together showed higher levels of conflict and less warmth than comparison children. In some cases this could be extreme.
- The first year of placement was reported to have been positive for most of the families' birth children.

- Specialist help for sibling relationship problems was rare.
- Social work help tended to be offered for children and parents separately.
- There was little evidence of direct work with the families' birth children.

References

Aldridge, M and Cautley, P (1976) 'Placing siblings in the same foster home', *Child Welfare*, LV:2 pp 85–93.

Dance, C for BAAF Adoption Statistics Project (1997) *Focus on Adoption: A snapshot of adoption patterns in England in 1995*, London: BAAF.

Bank, S (1992) 'Remembering and reinterpreting sibling bonds', in Boer, F and Dunn, J (eds) *Children's Sibling Relationships: Developmental and clinical issues*, Hillsdale New Jersey: Lawrence Erlbaum.

Bank, S and Kahn, M (1982a) 'Intense sibling loyalties', in Lamb, M and Sutton-Smith, B (eds) *Sibling Relationships: Their nature and significance across the lifespan*, (pp 251–266) New Jersey: Lawrence Erlbaum.

Bank, S and Kahn, M (1982b) *The Sibling Bond*, New York: Basic Books.

Barth, R and Berry, M (1988) *Adoption and Disruption: Rates risks and responses*, New York: Aldine de Gruyter.

Bellwood, P (1985) 'Assessing siblings for family placement', *Adoption and Fostering*, 9:3, pp 33–4.

Berridge, D and Cleaver, H (1987) *Foster Home Breakdown*, Oxford: Basil Blackwell.

Bilson, A and Barker, R (1992/93) 'Siblings of children in care or accommodation: a neglected area of practice', *Practice*, 6:4, pp 307–18.

Boer, F and Dunn, J (1992) *Children's Sibling Relationships: Developmental and clinical issues*, New Jersey: Hillsdale.

Boer, F and Spiering, S (1991) 'Siblings in foster care: success and failure', *Child Psychiatry and Human Development*, 21:4, pp 291–300.

Boer, F, Westenberg, P and Ooyen-Houben, M (1995) 'How do sibling placements differ from placements of Individual children?' *Child and Youth Care Forum*, 24:4, pp 261–69.

Brody, G, Stoneman, Z and Burke, M (1987) 'Family system and individual correlates of sibling behaviour', *American Journal of Orthopsychiatry*, 57:4, pp 561–569.

Brown, G (1983) 'Accounts, meaning and causality', in Gilbert, G and Abell, P (eds) *Accounts and Action*, Aldershot: Gower.

Bryant, B (1992) 'Sibling caretaking: Providing emotional support during middle childhood', in Boer, F and Dunn, J et al (eds) *Children's Sibling Relationships: Developmental and clinical issues*, Hillsdale NJ: Lawrence Erlbaum Ass Inc.

Bryant, B (1982) 'Sibling relationships in middle childhood', in Lamb, M and Sutton-Smith, B (eds) *Sibling Relationships: Their nature and significance across the lifespan*, New Jersey: Lawrence Erlbaum.

Bryant, B and Crockenberg, S (1980) 'Correlates and dimensions of prosocial behaviour: a study of female siblings with their mothers', *Child Development*, 51, pp 529–44.

Buhrmester, D and Furman, W (1990) 'Perceptions of sibling relationships during middle childhood and adolescence', *Child Development*, 61, pp 1387–98.

Cicirelli, V (1973) 'Effects of sibling structure and interaction on children's categorisation style', *Developmental Psychology*, 9, pp 132–39.

Cicirelli, V (1994) 'The longest bond: The sibling life cycle', in L'Abate, L (ed) *Handbook of Developmental Psychology and Psychopathology*, Wiley series on personality processes, NY USA: John Wiley and Sons.

Department of Health (1991) *Patterns and Outcomes in Child Placement*, London: HMSO.

Department of Health (2000) *Framework for the Assessment of Children in Need and their Families*, Department of Health.

Dunn, J and McGuire, S (1992) 'Sibling and peer relationships in childhood', *Journal of Child Psychology and Psychiatry*, 33:1, pp 67–105.

Dunn, J, Stocker, C and Plomin, R (1989) 'Assessing the relationship between young siblings: A research note', *Journal of Child Psychology and Psychiatry*, 31:6, pp 983–91.

Festinger, T (1986) *Necessary Risk*, Washington, USA: Child Welfare League of America.

Fratter, J, Rowe, J, Sapsford, D and Thoburn, J (1991) *Permanent Family Placement: A decade of experience*, London: BAAF.

Freud, A and Dann, S (1951) 'An experiment in group living', in Eisler, R (eds) *The psychoanalytic study of the child*, New York, USA: International Universities Press.

Furman, W and Buhrmester, D (1985) 'Children's perceptions of the qualities of sibling relationships', *Child Development*, 56, pp 448–461.

Graham-Bermann, S (1994) 'The assessment of childhood sibling relationships: varying perspectives on co-operation and conflict', *Journal of Genetic Psychology*, 155:4, pp 457–69.

Goodman, R (1994) 'A modified version of the Rutter Parent questionnaire including extra items on children's strengths: A research note', *Journal of Child Psychology and Psychiatry*, 35:8, pp 1483–94.

Groze, V (1996) 'A one and two year follow-up study of adoptive families and special needs children', *Children and Youth Services Review*, 18:1/2, pp 57–82.

Hindle, D (1995) 'Thinking about siblings who are fostered together', *Adoption and Fostering*, 19:1, pp 14–20.

Hodges, J and Tizard, B (1989) 'Social and family relationships of ex-institutional adolescents', *Journal of Child Psychology and Psychiatry*, 30:1, pp 77–97.

Holloway, J (1997) 'Outcome in placements for adoption or long-term fostering', *Archives of Disease in Childhood*, 76, pp 227–230.

Hoopes, J (1982) *Prediction in Child Development: A longitudinal study of adoptive and non-adoptive families*, New York, USA: Child Welfare League of America.

Jones, M and Niblett, R (1985) 'To split or not to split: the placement of siblings', *Adoption and Fostering*, 9:2, pp 26–29.

Kadushin, A and Siedl, F (1971) 'Adoption failure: a social work postmortem', *Social Work (USA)*, July, pp 32–38.

Kagan, R and Reid, W (1986) 'Critical factors in the adoption of emotionally disturbed youths', *Child Welfare*, LXV:1, pp 63–73.

Kier, C and Lewis, C (1998) 'Preschool sibling interaction in separated and married families: Are same sex pairs or older sister more sociable?', *Journal of Child Psychology and Psychiatry*, 39:2, pp 191–201.

Kosonen, M (1994) 'Sibling relationships for children in the care system', *Adoption and Fostering*, 18:3, pp 30–35.

Kosonen, M (1996) 'Maintaining sibling relationships – Neglected dimension in child care practice', *British Journal of Social Work*, 26, pp 809–22.

Lewis, K (1986) 'Sibling therapy with children in foster homes', in Combrinck-Graham, L (ed) *Treating Young Children in Family Therapy*, Rockville MD: Aspen.

Howe, D (1996) 'Attachment theory in child and family social work', in Howe, D (ed.), *Attachment and Loss in Child and Family Social Work*, pp 1–17, Ashgate Publishing Ltd.

Lord, J and Borthwick, S (2001, forthcoming) *Together or Apart? Assessing brothers and sisters for permanent placement*, London: BAAF.

Mapp, S (1995) 'Keep it in the family' *Community Care*, (12–18 January), p 25.

Millham, S, Bullock, R, Hosie, K, and Haak, M (1986) *Lost in Care: The problems of maintaining links between children in care and their families*, Aldershot: Gower.

Miller and Cantwell (1986) 'Siblings as therapists: a behavioural approach', *American Journal of Psychiatry*, 133, pp 447–450.

Morrison, T and Brown, J (1986) 'Splitting siblings', *Adoption and Fostering*, 10:4, pp 47–51.

Mullender, A and Kearne, S (1997) 'New thoughts on "other relatives" ', in *"I'm here waiting": Birth relatives' views on Part II of the Adoption Contact Register for England and Wales*, London: BAAF.

Nelson, K (1985) *On the Frontier of Adoption*, Washington, USA: Child Welfare League of America.

Nix, H (1983) 'Sibling relationships in older child adoptions', *Adoption and Fostering*, 7:2, pp 22–8.

O'Leary, S and Schofield, F (1994) 'The right of siblings to live together', *Practice*, 1, pp 31–43.

Parker, R A (1966) *Decision in Child Care: A study of prediction in fostering*, London: Allen and Unwin Ltd.

Pinderhughes, E (1996) 'Towards an understanding of family readjustment following older child adoptions: the interplay between theory generation and empirical research', *Child and Youth Services Review*, 18:1–2, pp 115–138.

Quinton, D, Rushton, A, Dance, C and Mayes, D (1998) *Joining New Families: A study of adoption and fostering in middle childhood*, Chichester: Wiley and Sons.

Quinton, D and Rutter, M (1984) 'Parents with children in care: current circumstances and parenting skills', *Journal of Child Psychology and Psychiatry*, 25, pp 211–30.

Raffaelli, M (1991) 'Conflict with siblings and friends in late childhood and adolescence', *Society for Research in Child Development*, Seattle WA:

Rosenberg, E (1988) 'Stepsiblings in therapy' in Kahn, M and Lewis, K (eds) *Siblings in Therapy: Life span and clinical issues*, New York, USA: Norton.

Rushton, A, Treseder, J and Quinton, D (1989) 'Sibling groups in permanent placements', *Adoption and Fostering*, 132:4, pp 47–51.

Rutter, M, Tizard, J and Whitmore, K (1970) *Education, Health and Behaviour*, London: Longmans.

Staff, I and Fein, E (1992) 'Together or separate: a study of siblings in foster care', *Child Welfare*, LXXI:3, pp 257–70.

Staff, I, Fein, E and Johnson, D (1993) 'Methodological issues in studying sibling placement', *Social Work Research and Abstracts*, 29:2, pp 35–7.

Stormshak, E, Bellanti, C and Bierman, K (1996) 'The quality of sibling relationships and the development of social competence and behavioural control in aggressive children', *Developmental Psychology*, 32:1, pp 79–89.

Taylor, E, Schachar, R, Thorley, G and Wieselberg, M (1986) 'Conduct disorder and hyperactivity 1: separation of hyperactivity and antisocial conduct in British child psychiatric patients', *British Journal of Psychiatry*, 149, pp 760–777.

Thoburn, J and Rowe, J (1988) 'A snapshot of permanent family placement', *Adoption and Fostering*, 12:3, pp 29–34.

Thorpe, M and Swart, G (1992) 'Risk and protective factors affecting children in foster care: a pilot study of the role of siblings', *Canadian Journal of Psychiatry*, 37:9, pp 616–22.

Timberlake, E and Hamlin, E (1982) 'The sibling group: a neglected dimension of placement', *Child Welfare*, 61:8, pp 545–52.

Trasler, G (1960) *In Place of Parents: A study of foster care*, London: Routledge and Kegan-Paul.

Ward, M (1984) 'Sibling ties in foster care and adoption planning', *Child Welfare*, 63:4, pp 321–32.

Wedge, P and Mantle, G (1991) *Sibling Groups in Social Work: A study of children referred for permanent substitute family placement*, Aldershot: Avebury.

Wedge, P and Phelan, J (1986) *Essex Child Care Survey (1981–85)*, Social Work Development Unit, Norwich: University of East Anglia.

Zill, N (1988) 'Behaviour achievement and health problems among children in stepfamilies: findings from a national survey of child health', in Hetherington, E and Arasteh, J (eds) *Impact of Divorce, Single Parenting and Step-parenting on Children*, Hillsdale, New Jersey: Lawrence Erlbaum.

Appendix

Demographic characteristics of sample and comparison families and matching procedure (Chapter 2)

Table A.1
Demographic characteristics of sample and comparison families
(excludes 19 sample families who were child-free prior to placement and had only one child placed with them)

Family characteristic	Sample (n = 53)	Comparison (n = 100)	Significance
Mean age of mother	39 (sd 7)	37 (sd 5)	F=10.9 (1,145) 0.001
Mean age of father	43 (sd 7)	41 (sd 7)	F= 8.5 (1,136) 0.004
Lone parent family	0%	15%	χ^2 = 8.9, df=1, 0.003
Minority ethnic group			
2 minority ethnic parents	0%	9%	χ^2 = 5.3, df=2, 0.071
Dual heritage family	8%	9%	
White family	92%	82%	
Occupational status (household)			
Professional or managerial	60%	47%	χ^2 = 7.9, df=3, 0.048
Clerical or retail	32%	27%	
Skilled or semi-skilled manual	6%	15%	
Unskilled manual	2%	11%	
Caring professions	37%	27%	n.s.
Family size			
2 children	47%	54%	n.s.
3 children	38%	35%	
4 children	13%	9%	
5 children	2%	2%	

171

The relationship between children's behavioural characteristics and poor parental evaluation of the placement at one year (Chapter 5)

Table A.2

Factors associated with poor parental evaluation of the placement at a year

	Single placements			Sibling groups		
Factor	*N*	*Poor Eval.*	*P*	*N*	*Poor Eval.*	*P*
Poor parent–child interaction						
None	20	19%	*	27	3%	**
Some placed children	–	–		8	25%	
All placed children	11	70%		2	100%	
Sibling interaction problems						
None	9	11%	*	24	4%	*
Some placed children	–	–		5	20%	
All placed children	4	75%		11	45%	
High behaviour score at 12/12						
None	15	13%	*	14	7%	n.s.
Some children	–	–		17	18%	
All children	14	50%		6	17%	

*Denotes group differences are significant at p<0.05 ** p<0.01 Group differences tested using Fisher's exact test for categorical data and Anova for continuous data.

Children's behaviour – itemised listing from Parental Accounts of Children's Symptoms (PACS) (Chapter 6)

Table A.3

Percentage of placed children with specific problems by age group 3 and 12 months into placement

Problem	0–4 yrs		5–10 yrs		11+ yrs	
	3/12	12/12	3/12	12/12	3/12	12/12
	(n=18)	(n=18)	(n=89)	(n=81)	(n=26)	(n=26)
Overactivity						
Concentration	45	39	43	28	23	30
Restlessness	39	33	37	27	15	33
Fidgets	22	39	30	36	22	38
Fiddling	17	22	22	30	20	33
Concentration in school	11	28	30	37	11	29
Conduct problems						
Lying	34	39	38	52	46	67
Defiant to parents	45	33	39	40	27	54
Defiant to others	6	6	17	9	15	21
Destroys own property	6	11	6	12	4	4
Destroys family property	6	11	7	12	23	17
Destructive outside	6	6	3	4	0	13
Stealing	6	11	13	18	12	21
Aggressive to peers	6	11	35	10	40	13
Teasing/bullying others	6	6	8	12	27	17
Firesetting	0	0	0	1	0	4
Cruel to animals	0	11	7	4	19	13
Emotional difficulties						
Eating	11	22	11	6	8	21
Sleeping problems	6	0	8	7	4	17
Fears	39	44	45	38	19	21
Worry	0	6	22	25	22	29
Chronic unhappiness	0	0	3	9	0	0
Interaction scale (not included in PACS)						
Response to pain	16	11	20	16	23	38
Comfort seeking	0	11	8	10	20	26

Problem	0–4 yrs		5–10 yrs		11+ yrs	
	3/12	12/12	3/12	12/12	3/12	12/12
	(n=18)	(n=18)	(n=89)	(n=81)	(n=26)	(n=26)
Lack spontaneous affection	0	6	10	10	15	29
Resistant to affection	0	6	6	5	15	4
Phoney affection	6	0	17	14	12	38
Unrelaxed physical contact	6	11	14	10	15	12
Doesn't differentiate parents	6	6	14	5	8	13
Over-friendly to strangers	40	23	49	28	12	33
Sexualised behaviour	6	11	27	29	23	38
Further items						
Fantasy	6	11	25	24	23	25
Irritable	22	6	28	28	42	38
Tempers	33	28	37	28	28	33
Headaches	0	0	1	0	8	4
Stomach aches	6	0	6	3	12	13
Pica (eating inedible objects)	22	28	21	14	0	8
Bedwetting	22	22	11	7	4	17
Soiling	11	6	10	6	7	8
Being teased/bullied	0	6	38	19	27	13
Believes people against them	6	0	16	5	11	4
Running away	0	6	12	10	0	4
Compulsive behaviour	6	6	6	1	12	17
Tics/twitches	0	0	1	0	4	13
Abnormal movements	0	6	10	7	4	13
Rocking	0	0	2	1	0	8
Self harm	11	6	6	10	0	8
Regression	28	11	24	32	18	13
Immature for age	11	6	22	34	15	25
Poor mastery	6	23	34	34	46	25
Pestering	11	22	19	16	17	13
Questioning	6	0	19	9	22	4

Notes to Table A.3: Scoring the PACS

The 35 PACS items provide an overall score of psychosocial difficulties (a maximum possible score of 35) along with three sub-scores for emotional difficulties (anxiety, worrying, fears and phobias, depression and the like); conduct problems (temper, defiance, fighting, lying and similar problems); and overactive and restless behaviour. The full set of items is given in Table A.3.

We used the data from the additional items to create a scale of difficulties in interaction with adults. The items included were: lack of age-appropriate comfort-seeking behaviour; an unusual response to pain or hurt; a lack of spontaneous affection, resistance to physical affection, displays of affection perceived by parents as non-genuine; a lack of differentiation of parents and over-friendliness towards strangers. Reliability analysis suggests that these items produce a reasonable scale, especially by 12 months (alpha for items at three months = .7 and .8 for items at 12 months).

Behaviour scores for singly and jointly placed children according to placement stability (Chapter 6)

Table A.4

Mean behaviour scores for singly and jointly placed children according to placement stability at one year

	Singly placed			Jointly placed		
	Stable 15 1	Less stable 10	Signifi- cance	Stable 79 1	Less stable 21	Signifi- cance
Overall score 3/12	5.9	7.3	–	5.3	6.2	–
Conduct score 3/12	1.4	2.0	–	1.2	2.0	–
Emotional score 3/12	0.7	1.2	–	0.8	1.1	–
Overactivity score 3/12	1.6	2.2	–	1.3	1.1	–
Interaction score 3/12	1.6	3.2	*	1.3	1.1	–
Overall score 12/12	4.8	9.7	**	5.8	6.5	–
Conduct score 12/12	1.1	3.1	**	1.6	2.4	–
Emotional score 12/12	0.8	1.4	–	0.9	0.7	–
Overactivity score 12/12	1.5	2.4	–	1.6	1.3	–
Interaction score 12/12	0.9	4.0	***	0.8	2.3	***

*p<0.05; **p<0.01; ***p<0.001.

Child-parent interaction difficulties according to context of emotional abuse (Chapter 6)

Table A.5
Level of interaction problems according to context of emotional abuse for whole sample, singly placed and jointly placed children

	None known	Emotional only	Emotional + sexual	Emotional + rejection +/- sexual	Total	Significance
			Type of Emotional Abuse			
Whole sample n=	**26**	**45**	**32**	**22**	**125**	
Parent–child interaction problem	8%	13%	28%	32%	14%	n.s.
Mean total interaction score 3/12	0.73	1.07	1.97*	2.08*	1.46	F=6.5 (3,116) p<0.001
Mean total interaction score 12/12	0.46	1.09	1.63*	1.95*	1.25	F=4.1 (3,121) p<0.01
Singly placed n =	**7**	**8**	**6**	**10**	**31**	
Parent–child interaction problem	0%	0%	50%	70%	33%	χ^2=14.5 (3) p<0.005
Mean total interaction score 3/12	1.14	1.38	1.83	2.23	2.1	F=3.2 (3,27) p<0.05
Mean total interaction score 12/12	0.29	0.63	2.17	3.90*	1.90	F=6.4 (3,27) p<0.005
Jointly placed n=	**19**	**37**	**26**	**12**	**94**	
Parent–child interaction problem	11%	16%	23%	0%	7%	n.s.
Mean total interaction score 3/12	0.61	1.00	2.00*	1.13	1.24	F=5.7 (3,85) p<0.005
Mean total interaction score 12/12	0.53	1.19	1.50*	0.33**	1.03	F=3.5 (3,90) p<0.02

*Mean score for this group is significantly higher than either no emotional abuse or emotional abuse only.
**Mean score for this group is significantly lower than either emotional abuse only or emotional and sexual abuse.
Significant differences determined using Tamhane's post hoc test.

Constellation characteristics of sample and comparison groups – matching criteria (Chapter 7)

Table A.6
Sibling group characteristics for placed sibling and new sibling constellations in comparison with the relevant comparison groups

	Placed sibling group n = 36	*Placed sibling control n = 39*	*New sibling group n = 13*	*New sibling control n = 18*
Age of eldest child				
Mean	9.2	8.8	12.8	12.7
Range	6–14	5–16	8–17	10–15
Sd. dev.	2.7	3.4	2.4	1.7
Age spread of group				
Mean	3.1	3.6	5.5	6.2
Range	1–6	0–6	1–10	3–9
Sd. dev.	1.6	1.7	2.6	1.8
Age gaps				
<1.5 yrs	80%	64%	31%	28%
1.5–2.5 yrs	20%	36%	54%	61%
>2.5 yrs	0	0	15%	11%
Gender mix				
All male	28%	13%	8%	0
Older male	25%	41%	46%	44%
Older female	28%	31%	38%	44%
All female	19%	15%	8%	11%
Family size				
2 children	56%	41%	38%	6%
3 children	36%	56%	46%	67%
4 or more	8%	3%	15%	28%

Table A.6 illustrates that, for both the placed and the new sibling groups, the matching procedure led to each sample sub-group and its relevant control sub-group being very similar in constellation characteristics.

Other publications on sibling placement from BAAF